GIDEON'S
PEOPLE

Carolyn Meyer

GIDEON'S PEOPLE

GULLIVER BOOKS

HARCOURT BRACE & COMPANY

San Diego   New York   London

Requests for permission to make copies of any part of
the work should be mailed to: Permissions Department,
Harcourt Brace & Company,
6277 Sea Harbor Drive, Orlando, Florida 32887-6777.

Gulliver Books is a registered trademark of
Harcourt Brace & Company.

Library of Congress Cataloging-in-Publication Data
Meyer, Carolyn
Gideon's people/by Carolyn Meyer
p.   cm.
"Gulliver Books."
Summary: Torn between youthful rebellion and their traditional
heritages, two boys from very different cultures—one Amish,
one Orthodox Jew—discover just how similar they really are.
ISBN 0-15-200303-7   ISBN 0-15-200304-5 (pbk.)
[1. Amish—Fiction.   2. Jews—United States—Fiction.
3. Family life—Fiction.]
I. Title.
PZ7.M5685Gi   1996
[Fic]—dc20   95-37917

Text set in Perpetua
Designed by Camilla Filancia
First Edition
A B C D E   A B C D E (pbk.)

Printed in Hong Kong

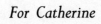

For Catherine

Lancaster County, Pennsylvania

Summer 1911

Lightning zigzagged across the sky, and thunder rumbled close by. A few drops of rain fell from the bunched-up clouds. A rickety wagon drawn by a sorry-looking horse reached the top of the lane, and a boy jumped down to open the gate. As the horse started through, a gust of wind yanked the gate out of the boy's hand, smacking the mare across the rump. She bolted, breaking the shafts of her harness and tossing the boy into the air and against a post. The driver dropped the reins and jumped off before the wagon rolled into the ditch and tipped over. Two of its wheels spun off in different directions.

Gideon was hurrying in from the field,

trying to beat the storm, when he saw the accident. He and his brothers, Amos and Levi, broke into a run. Datt jogged behind them, a little slower. There was another flash of lightning, and the rain let loose in a torrent.

Gideon could see the driver was Peddler Jakob, the only man Gideon knew of who drove such a run-down old wagon. The boy lay sprawled in the lane like he was dead, and the poor peddler looked scared half out of his wits.

Before Gideon could say anything, Datt caught up to them and gathered the boy in his arms like a newborn calf. He sent Gideon to chase after the mare. She moved pretty fast, considering the deep gash on her foreleg, and Gideon was drenched before he caught her. He coaxed her into the barn and wrapped a clean rag around the wound before he ran to the house.

Gideon found the boy laid out on a bed in the upstairs room kept for visitors. Gathered around him was the whole Stoltzfus family—Mamm, Datt, Amos, Levi, Annie, Ben, Danny, and little Katie.

In the midst of them, the peddler hung over the boy, wringing his hands and muttering. He talked so funny, half Dutch, half something else, a few words of English mixed in, with all kinds of arm waving. Gideon didn't catch all his words but he did understand that the boy's name was Isaac.

Gideon remembered how the peddler used to come around lugging a pack so big it must have been like carrying a cow on his back. Then he got himself a horse that looked like she was on her way to the glue factory, and he hitched her to a wagon ready for the kindling box. Gideon had joked with Levi that no Amish farmer would ever go out in such a rig. But Jakob sat up proudly on the driver's seat and handled that horse as though it was the finest money could buy, whistling as merrily as he always did. *Too bad about the wagon,* Gideon thought. But the main thing now was Isaac. He'd be all right, though. Mamm had taken over.

Isaac woke up on a strange bed in a strange house. Unfamiliar hands touched his arms, his legs, his head. He opened his eyes a slit. Unknown faces peered down at him. The hands belonged to a round-faced woman in a little white cap with strings tied under her chin. He focused on a girl with eyes the color of sky. She seemed to be upside down. The girl murmured something to her mother, and the mother replied, but Isaac couldn't catch what they were saying.

His eyes fell shut. With an effort Isaac opened them again. His father's troubled, black-bearded face loomed next to the girl's. "How do you feel, my son?" Tateh asked in a hoarse voice.

"Bad," Isaac whispered. He struggled to remember what had happened. One minute he'd been sailing through the air, and the next minute he'd slammed into the earth. Then nothing. "What happened to the wagon?" he asked through puffed lips. "What about Goldie?"

His father's frown deepened. "The wagon is wrecked," Tateh sighed, "and Goldie hurt her foreleg. But that is nothing. It is *you* I worry about."

"No need to worry," said the woman

with gentle hands. "No broken bones that I can find. Plenty of bruises, though, and some awful scrapes. His ankle and wrist are swoll up—sprained bad, I'd say. There's a knot on his head the size of an egg. But everything will heal in time."

She was talking about his body. He could hardly make out what she said. Some words made sense; others didn't. It was a different language from the Yiddish he spoke, yet like it somehow. He wondered what had become of his new hat, but then the thought flitted away.

"Bigger than an egg," said the blue-eyed girl. She wore a little cap like her mother's over her pale yellow braids. "More like an apple."

"Leave your boy with us, Peddler Jakob," said another voice, a man's. Isaac waited for the man's face to come where he could see it. A full red beard streaked with gray covered the man's chest, but his upper lip was clean-shaven. Wiry red eyebrows sprang out over hooded gray eyes. "We'll take care of him. He'll be good as new when you come back."

Or something like that. Isaac waited for

Tateh to say, "No, no, I will not leave him." But he didn't say it! Instead Tateh kissed his forehead and whispered, "Remember who you are, Isaac."

And instead of begging, Please do not leave me, Isaac said, "Yes, Tateh." It was because of Mameh and the new baby coming that he had to go; Isaac understood that.

He also understood what Tateh meant: *Remember that you are a Jew, Isaac, and the kind people who are caring for you are not Jews. Their ways are not our ways. Remember . . .*

Isaac's eyes closed again, and he drifted into sleep, away from the pain.

The storm passed, and the peddler went to see about his horse and wagon. Amos, the oldest brother, had to get home to his own farm to milk, but Gideon and Levi accompanied Jakob. The horse, like the boy, would mend. But the wagon was a sorry sight, lying in a ditch, bashed in and splintered, the boxes busted open, the merchandise scattered in every direction. They collected what they could, and later Jakob told Mamm to keep whatever they wanted of it in payment for taking in his boy.

Then Datt directed Levi to drive the peddler to Intercourse to get the trolley bound for Lancaster City, but Gideon jumped in and said, "I'll do it."

Levi grinned. "You want to show off your new rig." Datt had bought Lightning at auction in April and given him to Gideon, and that horse was the best in the barn, smooth as butter and fast as his name. Showing off was only a part of why Gideon was so eager, but he kept still until Datt shrugged and nodded. Gideon had Lightning hitched to his new buggy in no time.

Jakob brooded in silence as they raced along the muddy road. Gideon had a lot of questions he would have liked to ask the peddler who had done so much traveling—about trains going west from Lancaster, how much a ticket to Big Valley might cost—but the language differences made this kind of conversation too complicated, and so Gideon nursed his own thoughts. When they reached the trolley stop, the peddler thanked Gideon over and over in his mixed-up language, repeating how grateful he was that Mamm was taking care of his boy and promising to come back as soon as he could, in a week or so. "My wife looks for a new baby" is what Gideon thought he said.

"I'll do what I can for your horse," Gideon told him in Dutch.

"Goldie," Jakob said, and nodded sorrowfully.

Gideon left the peddler standing forlornly at the trolley stop, an odd figure in his long black coat, big black hat, and the thick black beard that nearly hid his lips. *The peddler's wife will sure be surprised when her husband comes home without the horse,* Gideon thought, *without the wagon, without the merchandise, and without the boy! Lucky nobody got hurt worse.*

Gideon drove to Huffnagle's General Store. He tied Lightning to the hitching rail and strolled inside, wishing he had a few pennies to buy something—a peppermint stick for his sister Annie, gumdrops for the younger ones. But he had nothing. The owner, white-haired Elmer Huffnagle, leaned on the counter. "What can I do for you, Gideon?"

"Thought maybe some mail was left here for me," he said, trying to act as though it was a matter of little consequence. "Gideon Stoltzfus," he added although he had been coming to this store ever since he was a boy.

Elmer checked a row of wooden boxes behind the counter, shuffling painstakingly through stacks of envelopes and newspapers while Gideon waited anxiously. "No, nothing today for Gideon Stoltzfus."

So there was nothing to do but go home again and hope that the next time he found an excuse to drive to Intercourse the letter he was waiting for would be there.

"You watch over the boy," Mamm said to Annie after she had stripped away his torn clothes and washed the dirt and blood off of him and dressed him in one of Datt's old shirts. "I'll make a poultice."

Mamm chopped a red beet up fine, heated the pulp, and tied it in cloths to lay on Isaac's cuts and bruises. She then sent Annie to the springhouse to wring out washrags in icy water to wrap around his swollen ankle and arm and over the knot on his head. When Mamm finally left, Annie settled herself on a chair by the bed and studied the boy.

She'd never met a boy like this Isaac. Long locks of dark hair straggled down in front of his ears. He and his Datt weren't what the Amish called *unser Satt Leit,* "our sort of people," and they sure weren't *englische Leit* like other *Englishers* she knew, but something else altogether. Jews, Mamm said, like in the Bible.

"They come from far away, across the ocean," she had explained, "persecuted and chased out by soldiers." Annie knew the Old Testament stories of Moses and Aaron in the wilderness, Joseph and Benjamin in Egypt, Abraham and Isaac. Quite a few Jewish peddlers came to the farm. One, a tall, skinny fellow, carried liniments and salves and ointments and cough syrup and corn plasters; another sold only eyeglasses; and there was the pots-and-pans man. Mamm liked this Jakob because he always gave extra measure when she bought cloth from him, and his prices were fair.

Annie always knew when Peddler Jakob was coming, because of his whistle. Today was the first time Jakob had brought the boy along. Isaac was sure banged up bad, and he was pale as death. He must hurt all over. Watching his chest rise and fall in a steady rhythm, Annie felt sorry that this had happened to them.

Annie's people usually talked English with *anner Satt Leit,* what they called "the other sort of people." But Jewish peddlers didn't talk much English. Annie could catch some of what they said but not all. It hadn't mattered much, until now.

Annie picked up the quilt she was

piecing and put her attention on that, waiting for the boy to wake up again.

Isaac dreamed of the *shtetl,* the Russian village his family had left four years earlier to come to America.

He dreamed of the spring Friday night, *Shabbes* night, that the Russians poured out of their churches, screaming, "Christ-killers! Christ-killers!" and beat up whatever Jews they could lay their hands on. A gang of Russian boys caught Isaac's grandfather, a rabbi, spit on him, and cut off his *payess,* his long earlocks.

"These *pogroms* will only get worse," Tateh had insisted when the terrible night was over. It was not the first such attack on Jews. The gentiles' hatred of them seemed to be spreading like a horrible disease. "We must leave here," Tateh concluded.

"But where can we go?" Mameh had sobbed.

"To the Golden Country! To America! Others have done it, and we will, too," Tateh replied. "We will start a new life for ourselves and the children, born and yet to be born."

At that time there were Isaac's sister Sarah, the eldest, then Isaac, and two younger sisters, Leah and Tirzah. Mameh was pregnant, but Isaac's parents believed they had plenty of time before the birth. They hadn't foreseen that the journey by cart to the port on the Baltic Sea would be so long and hard. Even after the family arrived at the docks, it took longer than expected to arrange passage. Isaac overheard their conversations in the night: Tateh arguing that they should return to the *shtetl* and attempt the journey later, after the baby was born, and Mameh resolutely insisting that they must keep on, that she could not bear to go back now that they had gotten this far. All of this was said in Yiddish, the only language Isaac spoke then.

Once aboard the steamer bound for America, Isaac's family found the passengers herded together like animals. The wild ocean storms were terrifying, and the food was disgusting—only tea and

moldy black bread and some salted fish—
but most of the time they were all too
sick to eat anyway. The sickness brought
Mameh's baby too early. The baby, so
tiny he fit in Tateh's cupped hands, lived
only a week and died before the steamer
reached America. An old woman gave
Mameh an embroidered linen pillowcase
to wrap the body, and Tateh gathered a
minyan, ten men, to recite the prayers for
the dead. Then the tiny white bundle was
let go overboard. Isaac watched it dis-
appear into the waves. Mameh cried and
cried. Nothing anyone said could console
her.

When at last they landed at Ellis Island,
Tateh had to carry Mameh ashore because
she was too weak to walk. Isaac and his
sisters struggled with the leather-bound
wooden trunk and the feather bed tied up
in a blanket, the only things they had
taken with them.

Isaac was too young then to realize all
that had been left behind or to imagine
all that lay ahead.

Now he opened his eyes, still trying to

straighten things out in his mind. He looked around the plain room—not even any curtains at the windows or pictures on the walls—and saw the girl. She sat on a straight chair at the foot of the bed, sewing. Isaac watched her for a while, until she saw him looking and laid down her work.

"Who are you?" Isaac asked, first in Yiddish and then in English.

"Annie," she said.

CHAPTER 2

The boy was watching her. He spoke to her in English.

"You hungry yet?" Annie asked him. "You've been asleep a good long while."

"Yes."

"I'll get you something to eat."

Annie went down to the kitchen. No one else was in the house. Mamm was in the springhouse with little Katie, skimming cream for churning. Annie's younger brothers, Ben and Danny, were in the vegetable garden pulling weeds and picking bugs off the tomato plants. Datt and Levi had gone back to work in the field after supper while there were still a few hours of daylight. Gideon had not yet come back from Intercourse.

Annie dipped up a bowl of bean soup from the pot on the cookstove and carried it upstairs. But the boy had fallen asleep again. Annie picked up her quilt patch.

The Nine Patch quilt called for twenty-four plain blocks and twenty-five pieced ones. Each pieced block was made of nine small square patches. Each pieced Nine Patch block was joined to a plain block, and then another Nine Patch, alternating plain and pieced, until you had a big square, seven blocks long and seven blocks wide. When it was finished, friends would be invited for a quilting party to sew the layers together with a pattern of fine stitches.

Her grandmother had started teaching her to make quilts when Annie was five, Katie's age, and hardly able to thread a needle or keep a thimble on her finger. Mawmy kept the scrap basket in the house built right next door to Annie's where she and Grossdawdy lived. Annie's first quilt, made for her doll, was all a jumble, pieced from whatever little odds and ends turned up. But for this Nine Patch quilt, to go in Annie's dowry chest, nicer scraps and odd pieces had been saved from the regular sewing. Dozens of patches were needed in several different colors and a plain border to go around all four sides.

In the center of each pieced block was a white patch, left over from making shirts for the men and boys. Some corner patches were deep blue and some green, from Mawmy's dresses. Annie's favorites were the color of grapes, from her own Sunday dress, and maroon, like red beets, from Katie's. For the plain gray blocks, Mamm got extra of the cloth she used to make everyday dresses, and Mawmy had promised to buy something special from the peddler for the border and the backing.

When the quilt was done, there would be something in it to remind Annie of everybody in the family: Mawmy and Grossdawdy and Mamm and Datt, of course; Amos, her oldest brother, who was married and farmed down the road; and the six Stoltzfus young ones still at home—Levi, aged nineteen; Gideon, sixteen; Annie herself, who was twelve; ten-year-old Ben; seven-year-old Danny; and finally Katie, five, the only girl besides Annie.

Mawmy taught Annie how to sew a quilt right, showing her when her stitches were not fine enough, not straight enough, not even enough. Gradually Annie improved. *"Sell iss Gut,"* Mawmy said. "That's good, Annie."

Annie yearned to add bright colors to her quilt. The deep shades in the quilt were the only ones allowed by their church. The colors Annie loved—rosy pink, sunny yellow and orange, and vivid blues and greens—were considered too worldly. Red was strictly forbidden, in clothes and in quilts. Red was the color of lust, Grossdawdy said, and of the devil. Annie was not certain what lust meant, but the devil she understood.

What Annie did *not* understand was why, if all those bright colors were worldly and therefore forbidden, did God make them in the first place? She loved the flame-colored geraniums that Mamm planted by the back door and the peonies blushing on the bushes in the front yard and the purply red petunias crowding the flower beds. Brilliant orange-and-yellow marigolds would bloom all around the barn in the fall, along with sunflowers and hollyhocks. All Annie had to do was step into the vegetable garden to observe more flaming color. In a few weeks the tomatoes would be red red red. Later there would be yellow squash and orange pumpkins big as her head. Peaches and apples would ripen in the fruit trees in all kinds of delicious colors. It seemed to Annie that every color she loved called attention to itself in God's creation. But none of them could be used in her quilt.

When Annie asked why, Mawmy only said, "Because the church elders forbid it." Mamm was no better help. "Can't you be content with what you have, Annie?" she said. "There are so many other pretty colors."

Some Amish church districts were more conservative than others, and their elders held to a stricter *Ordnung,* the rules of the church. Annie's family was Old Order Amish, the most conservative of all, opposed to any kind of change. Grossdawdy was a minister in their district. When the electric lines were brought out from Lancaster to run the trolleys and many *englische Leit,* English people, had power brought to their farms, Grossdawdy and the elders refused to consider such a thing.

There had been some trouble when Amos decided to marry Barbara King, whose father, Samuel, belonged to a church district known to hold liberal ideas. Samuel King was the first Amish in that part of the township to get a telephone, which caused quite a ruckus, even in his own church.

Annie understood why electricity and telephones were forbidden by most Amish. Her people were commanded to live separate from the world, as it said in II Corinthians. Datt read to them every week from their big German Bible: "Be ye not unequally yoked together with unbelievers; for what fellowship hath righteousness with unrighteousness? What communion hath light with darkness?" Having a telephone or electricity meant being yoked with the unbelievers who owned the utility companies.

But regardless of what the Bible said, and what the *Ordnung* of his church decreed, Samuel King had gone ahead and got a telephone. He built a little shed for it on the other side of his property line on land belonging to an *Englisher,* and he equipped it with a loud bell that he could hear from his house. When the elders of his church told him he had to take it out, he refused. Some of the others in that church district sided with Samuel, saying he had a right to a telephone, as long as it was on *englische* property. But in the end Samuel gave up and got rid of his telephone.

All of this happened while Amos was courting Barbara. Grossdawdy thundered, Datt fumed, but Amos was as bullheaded as they were. In the end he managed to convince them that he would not stray in a worldly direction and that he was actually leading his bride in more godly ways. It made for difficult wedding plans; they got married at Amos's home, instead of Barbara's, and Datt and Samuel King didn't have much to say to each other.

Not long after Barbara and Amos were married, Barbara was down with a bad cold and Mamm had sent Annie over with soup in a small tin kettle and a loaf of bread. On that day Annie saw with her own eyes her sister-in-law's quilt with a big red diamond in the center and four smaller red squares in the corners. "It's so pretty," she'd whispered to Barbara.

"I generally lay another one on top," Barbara confided, looking embarrassed that Annie had seen it. "Amos doesn't approve of this quilt, but it seems a shame to waste it. My old district didn't forbid using red. And I like knowing it's there, even when it's covered up. It cheers me." She hesitated. "The elders don't have to know every little thing we do. At least Amos agrees with me on that."

But Annie wasn't so sure. It seemed that the elders *did* know every little thing, and they had an opinion about it, too, if Datt was an example. It must have been hard, Annie thought, for Barbara to marry into Amos's strict family and have to take up all the ways of his church and give up her own. "If I ever had red," Annie said shyly, "I could not give it up for anybody."

Barbara laughed and blew her nose. "You'd find a way to keep it," she said. "Now you run along home, before you catch this cold." As Annie was leaving, Barbara had added, "But don't tell your Datt, all right? My sinful quilt is our secret."

Annie promised.

Now Annie concentrated on her dark-colored Nine Patch quilt, but hard as she tried, she could not keep her mind off another more disturbing secret, this one hidden under the bed where the boy Isaac lay. She'd known about it for a couple of days, since Mamm sent her upstairs to clean, saying, "Time to start getting ready for the preaching."

"It's not until Sunday after next," Annie had protested. "There's plenty of time yet."

"And there's plenty to do," Mamm chided.

Every other Sunday members of the church district gathered for the preaching in the home of one of the members. It worked out so each family took a turn about once a year. Annie's family's turn generally came in late spring or early summer. Cleaning the house from top to bottom was part of the preparation.

Annie did not see why she had to clean the upstairs floors because the preaching was held downstairs. Mamm reminded her that the elders always retired to an upstairs bedroom to pray before the service began, and so early Wednesday morning Annie had carried down the rag rugs and slung them over the fence.

Quilts were made from scraps of new cloth, but rugs were always made from worn-out clothes. The parts that could be salvaged were cut into long strips, the strips were braided, and the braid sewn together to form a circle, starting at the center and going around and around. The big oval rugs in the downstairs rooms were made of woolen strips, and the small round rugs beside each bed were from cotton rags. The trick was to keep the braids flat, so the rug didn't bunch up. The rug that lay next to Annie's bed, the first she'd made, bunched badly. But, as with quilts, she had gotten better at sewing rugs.

Wednesday forenoon Annie had swept the room that she shared with Katie, dunked her mop in soapy water, wrung it out, and swished it around the wooden floor. Next she swept and mopped the upstairs hall and continued into the room where Ben and Danny shared a big bed and Levi and Gideon each had their own narrow one. She finished with the spare room kept for visitors. By the time the family had had dinner and the dishes were put away, the floors were dry. Annie tucked up her skirt under her apron and got down on all fours. Slowly she worked her way up and down the wide pine boards in each room, rubbing them with a rag dabbed with beeswax, stopping now and then to rest.

By the time she'd gotten halfway across the spare room, her bare knees were sore and her back ached. She rested oftener and hurried to get done. Carelessly she ran the rag beneath the bed without looking—surely the elders wouldn't check under the beds when they came up here to pray, although Mamm might— and felt the cloth snag on something. She peered under the bed and gave the rag a yank. It ripped free of a nailhead that poked up from the floorboard and the board jiggled loose. Trying to shove it back in place, Annie noticed that the board next to it seemed loose, too.

Annie lay down flat and wriggled partway under the bed. Gingerly she lifted the loose board by the nail. It pulled up easily, and so did the one next to it, revealing a space between the joists under the floor. Annie groped blindly into the space, and touched something . . . cloth of some kind. She inched farther under the bed to see what it was and pulled out a pair of pants. She stuck her hand in again. The space seemed to be crammed with clothes. Still lying on her stomach halfway under the bed, she lifted them out and examined them.

They weren't Amish clothes. The pants had a fly front with buttons; Amish trousers had neither. This was a dress shirt and had a stiff collar; Amish Sunday shirts were collarless. She found forbidden store-bought suspenders, a flat cloth cap, even a necktie. She rubbed the necktie between her fingers. It had a slithery feel. *Silk,* she decided. Finally she pulled out a jacket with lapels and pockets and four large buttons down the front and rows of small buttons on the sleeves, all forbidden. Every single thing was taboo, prohibited by the *Ordnung,* just like electricity and telephones and the color red. *Englische* clothes. In one pocket of the jacket was a mouth organ. Musical instruments were forbidden, too.

Annie shuddered. Who did it all belong to? Levi? Gideon?

One more time Annie reached into the hiding place. This time her fingers closed on something firm and smooth—a book. She recognized it even before she read the title, *Treasure Island*. It belonged to Gideon.

Annie remembered a bitter cold March day two years earlier, when she and Gideon were walking home from school. Mamm had kept Ben at home for some reason—maybe he had a cold—and Danny hadn't started school yet. Gideon was fourteen and in the eighth grade, his last year of school. The sharp wind sliced right through Annie's thick woolen shawl. Annie was walking with the Beiler sisters, but Gideon kept falling behind. Annie had yelled, "Hurry up, slowpoke!" but it hadn't done a bit of good.

"You go on!" Gideon yelled back, and she did, keeping up with the Beilers but then dropping back to wait for Gideon after Becky and Lila turned off at their place. Gideon just kept poking along.

Gideon loved school. He wished it

lasted all year, he liked it that much—he'd even told her that. "I wouldn't mind going to school until I'm an old man," he said. He was not like Amos and Levi, who could hardly wait to get out and go to work on the farm full time with Datt. "Eight years in that schoolhouse is plenty," Amos said, and Levi said, "More than plenty," because he never did like school, even though Datt and Mamm said it was a good thing because they all needed to learn to read and write English and do their sums.

"You have to talk English good," Datt said. "When you go to the store, when you go to the market in town, if you have to go to the doctor, most *Englishers* don't talk Dutch."

The Amish called it Dutch, but according to Teacher, it was really *Deutsch*—German. Not German like they used for the preaching, but "a dialect," Teacher said. Annie wasn't sure what that meant. Teacher was *englische* herself, hired after the old teacher took sick.

Gideon caught on fast. He read all the

books Teacher had, even the ones for the older pupils. He'd helped Annie learn to read, too. Gideon was different from the rest of the family. *Dopplig,* Datt called him. Dreamy. That wasn't the only way Gideon was different: he was the only son who had not inherited Datt's flame-red hair. He was fair-haired, like Mamm and like Annie.

So Gideon had dawdled along that day until Annie noticed he was walking funny and asked him why. "Teacher gave me a book," he said. "I got it inside my clothes."

"Leave me see," Annie said.

He pulled the book out of his pants and showed it to her. The title, *Treasure Island,* was stamped in swirling gold script on the green cover with a name, Robert Louis Stevenson, beneath it. "Be careful," he warned her. "Don't get marks on it."

Annie opened the book and saw a beautiful colored picture of a fierce-looking man with a patch over his eye. She turned a few more pages and came across

drawings of other interesting-looking people. The book was not quite new, but it
was clean and none of the pages was torn
or missing.

"Is it to keep?" she'd asked.

"Yes."

She handed it back to him. "Datt won't
let you," she said.

"Why not?" Gideon asked, stuffing it
back in his pants, although he must have
already known the answer.

"Because it's worldly."

They'd looked at each other, and then
Annie looked away. "Will you tell?" he
whispered.

Annie shook her head, one small, quick
movement.

Neither of them ever mentioned the
book again. Annie never told anyone
about the book, because it would have
gotten Gideon in trouble, and she never
knew what happened to it. She would
have liked to read it, or at least look at
the pictures, even though they were
worldly. She thought Gideon must have
given it back to Teacher and in fact forgot

about it—until she found it in the hidey-hole with the *englische* clothes.

Those *englische* clothes scared Annie. Gideon had hidden them there for a reason—but what could it be? Maybe he wanted them so he could sneak off and be wild someplace, believing if he was dressed up in those clothes nobody would know he was Amish. Annie had heard about other boys doing this. But Gideon wouldn't get away with that because of his hair. All Amish boys and men wore their hair down over their ears. Annie herself had sometimes cut Gideon's hair, snipping straight across the back, even with the bottom of his ears and straight across his forehead. Even with *englische* clothes everybody would look at Gideon's hair and know. So it wasn't just for raising Cain that he had the clothes.

Far worse than that: maybe it meant that Gideon planned to leave. Every so often it happened, although nobody talked much about it. One of Mamm's cousins had lost a son that way—he cut his hair, put on an *englische* suit, and went to work for the railroad. His family never spoke his name again; it was as though he never existed. She could not begin to imagine how it would be if Gideon did such a thing.

Then she felt a faint flutter of hope. Suppose the clothes and the mouth organ belonged to one of Gideon's wild friends—Jonah Byler, perhaps, or more likely Crist Miller, who was always up to some devilment.

Annie folded the clothes the way she thought they'd been and stuffed them back into the hiding place on top of *Treasure Island*. Numbly she set the boards in place and wriggled out from under the bed. She had to talk to Gideon and ask him why he had the forbidden clothes and pray that he had some simple explanation.

But it was two days since she had found the hidey-hole and the clothes, and there had been no chance to talk to Gideon alone. Mostly he was out in the field with Datt and Levi all day, and at mealtimes and in the evening before the family went to bed, there was always somebody around. Now he was in Intercourse, taking Peddler Jakob to the trolley. The discovery was on her mind nearly every minute.

For the last two nights Annie hadn't slept very well. Every time she closed her eyes, she pictured Gideon. Gideon, taking her for the first ride in his new buggy and letting her handle the reins. Gideon, speaking up for her when Datt got mad because she'd asked too many questions. Gideon, leaving forever. Twice she got up in the night and peeked in the boys' room hoping Gideon was awake, but he and the rest were sound asleep. *How can he sleep?* she wondered. Now Annie couldn't stand it when she didn't know just where Gideon was. He was her favorite of the whole family, and she couldn't bear the thought of him leaving.

She knew she ought to tell Mamm about what she had found, but Mamm was sure to tell Datt, and then Datt's temper would fly. If she told, it would just get Gideon in trouble.

Yesterday Annie had run into Levi on the way back from the outhouse, and she'd had the notion of blurting it out to him: "I'm afraid Gideon wants to run away. What can we do?" But she didn't tell Levi, either. Since Levi got baptized last year and was the oldest son still at home, he'd turned so sober it would be like talking to Datt, stern and unyielding.

Finally Annie thought of Barbara and the red patches on her quilt, kept secret from the rest of the family. Barbara had said, "The elders don't have to know every little thing we do." Barbara would keep another secret. She would come with Amos and the baby on Sunday, and Annie would ask her advice.

Annie bit off another length of thread and studied the sleeping boy, her needle darting in and out of the somber patches. This boy with the long locks of dark hair was *anner Satt Leit,* a Jew from some far-away place. He must know about the world, much more than she did. When he woke up, she would ask him to tell her about it. Then, when Gideon got back, she would find a chance to talk to him.

CHAPTER 3

Again Isaac dreamed:

It was Friday. As the sun slid down the bowl of the sky toward the start of the Sabbath, his family counted the take. Isaac and his sisters hitched their stools closer to the kitchen table as Tateh pulled the canvas bag from the secret pocket stitched inside his long black coat and spilled the coins out on the table.

His sisters counted, and Isaac wrote down the numbers and added them up. He was twelve and good with figures; Tateh called him "our accountant." Then Mameh doled the coins into a row of mismatched china cups—so much for the rent, so much for food. The money in the cup with the chipped rim was for more goods for Tateh to peddle to Amish farmers.

There was also a cup to save up for other necessities, like shoes and coal, and some set by for "just in case." Now "just in case" was the new baby Mameh expected in June. And always a little something went into the *pushke,* the cup for charity.

Whatever was left over—*if* anything was left over—Mameh tied up in a woolen stocking that she hid in a wooden trunk by her bed. They called it the Dream Stocking. They were saving up to buy a horse and wagon. A dream wagon.

After the ritual of the counting, they got ready to welcome *Shabbes,* the Sabbath. Dressed in their good clothes, they gathered again around the kitchen table, covered now with a white cloth and set with two candles, the precious silver wine cup carried across the sea from their old home, and two shiny brown loaves of *challah,* the special braided bread Mameh always baked for the Sabbath. At the moment the sun slipped behind the roofs,

Mameh lit the candles, covered her eyes with both hands, and recited a prayer in Hebrew: "Blessed art Thou, O Lord our God, King of the Universe, who sanctified us by his commandments and bid us to kindle the Sabbath lights." When she uncovered her eyes, the Sabbath had begun.

When Isaac awoke he noticed a peculiar smell drifting up from the kitchen. He couldn't figure out what it was—definitely not something Mameh made. He thought he might be hungry, but not for whatever was making that odd smell. *Later,* he thought and slept again.

Every Sunday afternoon Tateh packed up for the week's peddling. In the old days, before the wagon, he had spread a piece of striped bedticking on the kitchen table. He laid on it two or three bolts of unbleached muslin, followed by a layer of dress goods in plain colors: indigo blue, rich purple, wine red, dark green, plain black. No pink cloth, no bright red, no checked gingham, no dots or stripes, no flowers. "It is the religion of my Amish customers," Tateh explained. "Plain things only."

On top of the cloth he set a box of many compartments filled with notions—packets of hooks and eyes, pins and needles, thimbles and scissors, combs and brushes, pocketknives, razors, lead pencils, and only a few buttons.

"Amish do not use buttons," Tateh had told them when he came home from his first trip, bringing back as many buttons as he had started out with. Buttons had been a proven seller in the past when they lived in New York; everybody there needed buttons.

"No buttons?" Mameh asked, baffled.

"None on women's dresses, none on men's coats, only sometimes on shirts. Again, it is their religion."

"What have buttons to do with religion?"

"I do not understand it either," Tateh said, "but Amish people do not believe in any kind of modern progress. They call it the work of the devil. To most of them buttons are modern, and somehow associated with the military, so they use hooks and eyes to fasten their clothes. There are other strange things as well. Beards, but no mustaches—do not ask me why. And never call them Mister or Missus or any such title, but only by their given names. Every day I learn something new about my customers."

More items went on top of the notions box, and then Tateh folded the mattress ticking over the pile and secured the bundle with leather straps fastened to a harness. He knelt on the floor and Mameh helped him get his arms into the harness. He struggled to his feet, hoisting the enormous pack onto his back. Tateh was not a big man, and the pack was the size of a cookstove and might have weighed more than he did. Mameh straightened his black hat and touched his cheek. The girls tiptoed up to kiss him good-bye, careful not to unbalance him.

"One of these days," he said, as he had every week for the three years they had lived in Lancaster, "I shall buy a horse and wagon." They knew it like a prayer.

On a blustery Sunday a couple of

months earlier, Isaac had accompanied his father, as he always did, to Penn Square, where all the trolley lines converged. Tateh had sketched a rough map of his territory, tracing the trolley routes that fanned out from the square and marking the villages they passed through: Bird-in-Hand, Blue Ball, Intercourse, Paradise, White Horse, Gap. A chill wind was blowing. Tateh would do no business that day—the Amish didn't trade on their Sabbath—but usually a hospitable farmer would allow him to sleep in the barn that night.

When he had found the right trolley, Tateh patted Isaac on the head and hauled himself and his pack aboard. The bell clanged, sparks crackled from the overhead wires, Isaac waved, and the trolley lurched down the track.

The next Friday afternoon Isaac and Sarah had waited on the front stoop, as they always did, stamping their feet to keep warm and listening for a familiar whistle in the distance. But instead of Tateh striding along under his pack, they saw a wagon drawn by a plodding horse, and holding the reins was Tateh, his whistle trilling like a bird's.

For the three years they had had the Dream Stocking, Isaac had pictured a horse with a sleek coat, a silky mane, and a long, swishing tail. The wagon would be satiny black, the spokes of the wheels painted red, the driver's seat padded with smooth leather. JAKOB LITSKY AND SON, DRY GOODS AND NOTIONS would be lettered in gold with fancy curlicues on the sides of the wagon. Isaac would travel with his father, and someday he would be a peddler with a horse and wagon of his own.

This wretched animal was bony and knobby-kneed. Her back sagged, her head drooped, and her mane was as thin as a worn-out broom. Even worse was the wagon. The iron wheels were rusty, the paint chipped and faded, some of the sideboards were cracked or missing altogether. The driver's seat was a narrow plank, warped and splintered.

Tateh leaped down from the wagon

seat, calling out, "Well, my darlings, what do you think? Is it not wonderful?"

It is awful, Isaac thought, but he forced a smile. "Yes, Tateh," he lied through clenched teeth. "It is wonderful."

The front door flew open and Mameh stepped out. She stopped short and folded her hands across her round belly.

"I got it at a good price, Esther," Tateh said. "The most for the money. But it took almost every cent I had."

Surely, Isaac thought, *she is as disappointed as I am at what Tateh brought home.* But Mameh beamed and said as though she really meant it, "It is a beginning, Jakob. An excellent beginning."

The younger girls squeezed past Mameh and rushed out to look. They fussed over the horse, agreed that she should be called Goldie because of the color of her coat, and clamored to be taken for a ride in the wagon. They didn't seem disappointed at all! And Sarah was squealing louder than anybody! Did she really like it as much as she seemed to, or was she just pretending for Tateh's sake?

"Once around the block, ladies," he said. Isaac's sisters scrambled into the wagon bed. "And you, Isaac?" So Isaac climbed in, too, annoyed that he was expected to sit in back with the girls. But at least none of his friends was likely to see him there.

As the wagon jolted over the cobblestones, Isaac considered the situation. This certainly wasn't what he'd call a "dream wagon." He was disappointed, embarrassed even, but he still wanted to go peddling with his father. So what if it wasn't the best-looking rig? Having the real thing was much better than dreaming about it. First he had to persuade Tateh to take him along, and then he had to persuade Mameh to let him go. Tateh, he was sure, would be pleased. Mameh wouldn't. He knew exactly what she'd say: "One peddler in the family is enough. For you, Isaac, something else. A better life. An *easier* one."

No sense arguing about it now, Isaac had decided before the ride around the block was over; better to wait until school was out for the summer to make his plea.

Then Sarah crept over next to him and whispered in English, "It's ugly, isn't it?" She burst out laughing.

"It's not so bad," Isaac had said, already beginning to believe it.

Isaac awoke, thinking of Goldie. *Hurt her foreleg,* he'd heard Tateh say. *But it is you I worry about.* Then left. Left him and Goldie behind. Because of the baby, that was why. Isaac understood that. But he hurt, and the smells from this unfamiliar kitchen were so strange. What would he find to eat here? He slipped back into his dream.

Spring had passed slowly, dragging its muddy feet. When Tateh came home on weekends, talk around the supper table often centered on Isaac's *bar mitzvah,* to take place in September at the time of his thirteenth birthday. Isaac was excited about this ceremony, but there was a negative side: he must continue to study all summer at *cheder,* the Hebrew school, to learn to read from the Torah, the sacred scrolls. Both his parents would think studying was more important than Isaac going along with his father. But Isaac had an argument ready for that: he would take his books along to study as they traveled.

On the last Friday in May, which was also the last day of school, the family had gathered around the kitchen table for the weekly ritual. The sack of coins was heavy that day, and after Mameh counted them into the cups, there were still a few left over. Isaac seized the moment. "Please take me with you next week, Tateh. I will be a big help—you will make even more money!" Should he mention his plan to study Hebrew on his own? He decided it might be better not to bring it up just yet.

Tateh and Mameh looked at each other, but they didn't answer. It was time to light the Sabbath candles. The meal was eaten, the candles burned down, and still there was no answer—none that night or the next morning. During Saturday dinner Tateh told stories about the farms he had visited, the people he had met, how obedient Goldie had been. Isaac waited in an agony of impatience. *Now,* surely, they would tell him what they had decided!

But no—when the meal was over, his parents yawned deeply and went off to take their customary Sabbath nap. Isaac sat on the stoop, preparing his arguments in case they said no.

While he waited, willing the time to pass, Abie Siegel came by to visit. Abie had been his friend since fourth grade, when Isaac's family had moved to Lancaster from New York City, two months after the start of the fall term. The Siegels had come from Russia as well, but from a different part than Isaac's family; Abie's father was a peddler who bought and sold old clothes and rags. Abie's family had lived in Lancaster for over a year when Isaac arrived, and Abie knew the ropes.

"This isn't like New York where all the kids are Jews," Abie had told him. "Here there's gentiles, too." The gentiles here weren't so bad, in Abie's opinion, not like the Russian gentiles. But Abie had advised Isaac to watch out for the German Jews who had lived in Lancaster so long they thought they were better than the new immigrants from Russia. "Don't let those other Jews hear you talking Yiddish," Abie warned him. "They'll make fun of you."

Everything would have been a lot harder for Isaac if it hadn't been for Abie.

"What're you hangin' around here for?" Abie demanded, still in English. Another reason Abie spoke English was so adults wouldn't understand. "Let's go do somethin'."

"Can't." Isaac jerked his head toward the house. "I'm waiting for them to wake up and tell me if I can go with Tateh."

"You think they'll let you?"

"I don't know. They might make me stay home and go to *cheder*."

Abie nodded sympathetically. "Yeah. I gotta go, too, and I hate it. Reb Horowitz stinks of garlic, and he smacks you across the knuckles when you make a mistake. Lucky you, if you can get out of it."

At last the sun disappeared behind the jagged rooftops, the Sabbath ended, and

Abie sauntered home. Once again Isaac's parents sat at the kitchen table, drinking tea and talking business: How much of this or that should be ordered? Was that the best price, or could it be gotten cheaper elsewhere?

His patience exhausted, Isaac sighed loudly, took a lantern from the back porch, and ran to the shed Tateh had rented from a neighbor down the block. He spoke softly to Goldie, and she nuzzled his palm. He had grown almost fond of her, homely as she was. The wagon loomed in the shadows. It didn't appear so decrepit in the dim light. Isaac hung the lantern on a hook and climbed up onto the seat. "Giddyap, Goldie," he said and clucked his tongue and flicked invisible reins, imagining himself traveling through the countryside. He would learn to whistle.

"Whoa!" Tateh stepped out of the shadows and into the circle of yellow light. "Tomorrow you will help me load the wagon," he said. "We shall leave after dinner." But then he held up his hand and added, "But for one week only. Then you are back to *cheder* to study Hebrew. I promised Mameh."

Mameh had made a list of every item, which Tateh was supposed to mark off as they were sold. She could neither read nor write; instead she drew symbols: a circle with a line through it meant a bolt of cloth; a big **X** meant scissors; two little slanted lines **//** were for a paper with a half dozen needles, and three lines **|||** were for a packet of three dozen pins.

But Tateh never remembered to mark off his list, claiming he kept it all in his head. That wasn't good enough for Mameh. "You are the accountant now, Isaac," she said as they began packing the wagon for the week. "In charge of inventory."

One of the wagon boxes was fitted out for their personal use: a little spirit stove, a tin pot, plates and cups. Mameh wrapped leftover potato kugel in a clean cloth for their supper. Isaac prepared his bedroll, a blanket with a change of clothes packed inside and an oilcloth tied around it in case of rain. As they were about to leave, Mameh gave Isaac a gift, a hat like Tateh's, black and wide-brimmed.

"When you come home next Friday, there may be a new brother or sister waiting for you," Mameh said and kissed Isaac on both cheeks.

"You are sure that you will be all right?" Tateh asked her anxiously, squeezing her hand.

"I shall take good care of Mameh," Sarah announced. "And the baby, too."

"We will be fine," Mameh assured them. "But watch what he eats, Jakob," she begged. "Isaac does not know *treyf*." *Unclean,* she meant, *not kosher.* Meat from an unclean animal, like pork, or meat not slaughtered according to the strict rules observed by Orthodox Jews, was *treyf*.

Mameh's warning annoyed Isaac. Of course he knew *treyf*! Abie had often dared him to buy a frankfurter or a ham sandwich from one of the vendors at Central Market. "You go first," Isaac had told Abie, but Abie always weaseled out. "I already ate it lots of times. There's nothing to it. It's your turn." But the thought of the unclean food made Isaac sick, and then he had to weasel out. Now Isaac reassured his mother, "I will be careful, Mameh."

"Do not worry," Tateh told her. He and Isaac climbed up onto the wagon seat. "We will make out fine together, will we not, Isaac?" Tateh winked and clucked at Goldie.

Treyf, Isaac thought, waking up. That's what he was smelling. The food in this Amish house was *treyf,* and he would starve.

CHAPTER 4

With barely a touch of the buggy whip, Lightning streaked over the rutted roads, splashing through puddles and spraying up twin plumes of water. Gideon gave his horse free rein all the way home from Intercourse, although the way things were between him and Datt, Gideon himself was in no hurry to get there.

Watching Lightning's muscular rump, smooth as polished wood, Gideon pondered again what would become of his horse, once the letter arrived and Gideon knew for sure when he was going away. He would leave his open one-seater buggy behind for Ben, that much he'd decided, although he'd much rather give it to Annie. Wouldn't that get Datt's goat! Too bad girls didn't have buggies, or he'd do it. But in a few years Ben would be old enough for running around, and he'd need one. Besides, Datt had paid for the buggy, so it really belonged to him and in the end he'd be the one to decide.

Datt had paid for Lightning, too, but after two years of working for no wages, ever since he'd left school at the end of eighth grade, Gideon felt he had earned that horse. If he decided to sell Lightning, he would have no trouble finding a buyer. His friend Crist said he knew somebody who'd give him more for the horse than Datt had paid for it, and the money would help out a lot.

Gideon didn't know exactly when he would go away, but he hoped it would be soon—maybe when the harvest was over, so he wouldn't feel bad about leaving his share of the work for Levi. There was no such thing as a good time to leave. Mamm would cry her eyes out and Datt would be mad as a hornet. Mawmy would shake her head and pray for his salvation, and Grossdawdy would thunder that he'd gone to the devil. Amos and Levi would be shocked and upset and might even vow to come after him, and the little kids would certainly miss him. Then they'd all get over it when they realized he wasn't coming back.

Annie was a different matter. It was Annie that bothered Gideon most. He hated the thought of leaving her. He'd thought about taking her with him, but that was impossible. He couldn't ask her to leave, and he could not do that to his family. It would be like a funeral when they realized he was gone, and it would be double grief if Annie were to go, too. Gideon knew he'd likely never see her again, and that pained him more than anything.

Gideon thought about his reasons for leaving. He had a couple, but the one that mattered most was that he just couldn't seem to get along with Datt, no matter how he tried. Not like Levi and Amos did, like Ben and Danny would someday, all redheads like Datt and alike in other ways as well. But Gideon was always different. Nothing he did seemed good enough, and it had gotten so he didn't feel much like trying. More and more he let his mind go elsewhere, away from the farm, to places he had read about. Naturally that made Datt madder than ever. Datt's famous temper was always seeking out Gideon, the way lightning seeks a tree or a barn. Amos, now a married man with a beard and a new baby, had even come over back in the spring and tried to talk to Gideon about how things were going with Datt. Amos said it was all up to Gideon, that he had to try harder. But that just made Gideon mad at Amos, too. Amos didn't understand—or else he pretended not to.

"Do what Datt says and don't argue," Amos advised. "I did it; Levi does it. You got to do it, too. Five or six years from now you'll be off on your own anyway."

Five or six years! That seemed like half a lifetime to Gideon. He could not stand to think of working day after day, year after year, for a man who seemed to have so little regard for him, who thought he was *dopplig*.

"Besides," Amos had reminded him, "you don't have a choice, Gideon. Has Datt talked to you about getting baptized?"

"Sure he has," Gideon admitted. "Both him and Dawdy." Datt and Grossdawdy were always after him to settle down and join the church, but Gideon wanted no part of it. "I just told them I'm not ready. I explained it's better not to take the vow in the first place than to break it later on. There wasn't much to argue with that."

"It's not so bad," Amos said. "You'll see. Just ask Levi. He'll tell you."

"He has already."

Levi had been baptized last September, and ever since that day it seemed that he had changed and had started taking everything more seriously. Levi seemed to be keeping an eye on Gideon, ready to find fault almost as much as Datt did.

"Sooner or later," Levi said, "you have to do it. Everybody does. Better make up your mind to it."

Everybody does. Next it would be Gideon's turn to be baptized into full membership in the church. Datt talked about it, Grossdawdy lectured him, the ministers all turned their eyes on him during the preaching. It was not that Gideon wanted to run around and be wild, like Crist was, and like Amos once did—oh, him and that Barbara! Gideon knew they danced before they got married and maybe even for a while after, and Amos thought he'd kept it a secret. But people gossiped. Levi had been even worse—he'd smoked cigarettes and got beer from some *englische* boys. Then he started keeping company with Nancy Esh and she found out about it and threatened to break off with him and tell Datt on him if he didn't quit. Next thing Gideon knew, Levi agreed to get baptized, and now he was worse than the preachers. It was hard to see a brother, somebody you thought you knew, change so much.

"You'll be wanting to get married one of these days," Amos had told him, "and you know they won't let you get married if you haven't been baptized. I don't blame you for wanting to sow some wild oats first, everybody does, but then you have to get serious. And marriage is a good thing, too." He smiled at Gideon. "You don't know what you're missing."

But Gideon didn't want to sow wild oats and marriage was still a long way off. He knew Lizzie Esh, Nancy's sister, had eyes for him, but he wasn't that interested in her. At least he wasn't interested enough to take the first step and get baptized. Maybe he wouldn't ever be. And it wasn't that he couldn't accept Jesus Christ as Lord and Savior; he did. And as far as sowing wild oats was concerned, beer gave Gideon a headache and cigarettes made him dizzy. It was promising to accept the *Ordnung* and never to depart from it; never to sit down and read *Treasure Island,* if he wished; never to play a tune on the mouth organ if he felt like it, that was the problem.

Once you were baptized—once you took the vow to forsake the world, the flesh, and the devil—then you were a member of the church and the days of freedom were over. No more running around, no more wildness. Until then, running around was to be expected, although Gideon could not imagine Datt ever being wild, let alone Grossdawdy. But the end of such freedom didn't bother Gideon as much as something else. After you were baptized, if the church elders found out you were doing something they didn't like, something against the *Ordnung*—the church rules—then you could be punished with the *Meidung,* the shunning. Gideon had witnessed it.

Three summers before, Datt's brother Aaron had cut his hair a little too short. Nobody knew why. The elders criticized Aaron for it and told him he had to let it grow out at least an inch and keep it that length. Aaron was kind of hot-tempered, like Datt, and the elders made him mad. Aaron had told the elders that if they wanted something to criticize, he would give them something to criticize. He took off his hat, grabbed a knife, and whacked off more than an inch all the way around the brim. This made his hat a full inch narrower than the *Ordnung* called for. That really did it! Aaron stubbornly refused to get rid of the hat or to grow his hair longer, and so the elders put him under the ban and shunned him. Nobody was permitted to speak to Aaron, not his own brothers and sisters—not even his oldest boy, Zeke, who was already baptized. The elders tried to make Aaron's wife, Lydia, shun him, too. But she refused. So they put her under the ban and shunned her as well. This was a year before Grossdawdy was made a minister, but even so he was just as stern as everybody else, against his own son.

Gideon was thirteen when that happened. He remembered very well how bad everybody felt. It was like Aaron was dead, and Lydia, too. Datt and Grossdawdy and Mawmy and all the relatives grieved, but they wouldn't forgive Aaron's refusal to conform. So Aaron packed up and moved his family, except for the oldest boy, clear out near Belleville in Big Valley—more than a hundred miles from Lancaster County—to get away from the *Meidung* and start over in a new place. All for an inch of hair and an inch of hat brim!

Gideon probably felt worse than anybody when they moved. Aaron was Gideon's favorite uncle. Aaron was a lot like Datt, even down to the fiery temper, but somehow Gideon and Aaron got along in ways he and Datt didn't, and in ways that Aaron didn't get along with his own son, Zeke. Before Aaron left, he took Gideon aside and told him that if he ever wanted to get away, he should come out to Big Valley and Aaron would take him in and give him work. "You'd be welcome with us," his uncle said.

That had started Gideon thinking. But he was only thirteen then and still had another year of school. Sometimes he'd manage to push it out of his mind for a while. But the next year school was finished and Gideon and Datt were together all the time. It didn't take much for them to get into an argument that inevitably blew up into a fight. The fights always ended with Datt giving Gideon a smacking with a buggy whip. And that would start Gideon thinking all over again about leaving.

Then, less than a month ago, Aaron and Lydia had come back because Lydia's father had taken sick and died. Lydia's brother, who belonged to a different church district, kept in touch. He had sent them the news. Some people in Gideon's district still shunned them, but others said it was different now because Aaron's family had moved away and joined another church district and was no longer subject to their *Meidung*. Datt was one of the strict ones. He still refused to talk to his own brother. But Gideon heard about their visit and sneaked off to see his aunt and uncle anyway, without letting on to Datt.

"When are you coming out?" Aaron asked Gideon. Aaron told him all about their farm in Big Valley and how their new district didn't have the same strict *Ordnung* as Datt's and Grossdawdy's. The hats out there in his new district had a

66

narrow brim that looked almost *englische,* and people buttoned their clothes. "You might like it out there," Aaron said, and Gideon agreed. Maybe he would. "Just as nice as here but more modern."

For several days Gideon turned the idea over and over in his mind. It wasn't the more liberal *Ordnung* that drew him, although the notion of being "modern" was intriguing. The idea of farming with Aaron, who seemed to appreciate him so much more than Datt did, was a powerful lure.

Somehow Datt found out that Gideon had defied him and gone to see Aaron anyway. Gideon suspected that Levi had heard about it and told. "You have the devil in you!" Datt had roared. And Gideon had roared back, the first time he had openly defied his father. Datt had hauled him out behind the barn and given him the smacking of his life, even though Gideon was nearly as big as Datt was. Gideon had taken the smacking—it had not occurred to him that he could have wrenched the whip out of his father's hand. But he made up his mind right then: *I'm going. And there's nothing you can do to stop me.*

When Gideon went to find his uncle to tell him his decision, Aaron and his family had already left for Big Valley. It took all of Gideon's courage to visit Lydia's brother John and ask for Aaron's address. He was glad that John didn't ask any questions but simply wrote it out for him on a slip of paper and handed it to him. The next time Gideon had an excuse to drive into Intercourse, he bought paper, an envelope, and a stamp from Elmer Huffnagle and sat on the bench outside to write his message: "I am ready to come. Write to me in care of Huffnagle's store and tell me how to get there." He signed his name, folded the paper, sealed the envelope and stamped it, then drove home in a state of exhilaration.

Now he waited for a reply, which still had not come.

If he sold Lightning, Gideon thought now as he got closer to home, he'd have money for the train fare to Mifflin County and then some. But he knew the horse wasn't his to sell, any more than the buggy was. Lightning belonged to Datt. Gideon would have no choice but to get a job in Lancaster City for a week or two until he had enough for the train ticket. He'd have to raise the money on his own. The idea seemed like an adventure.

Meantime, so he'd be ready when the time came, Gideon had bought some worldly clothes from some *Englisher* his friend Crist knew. He'd taken the money Amos's wife, Barbara, had given him when he built a little picket fence around her flower garden and got himself trousers with cuffs and a button fly, a silk necktie that he didn't know how to tie, and a cap that looked dumb with his Amish haircut. But he'd fix that. These clothes were hidden in the secret place where he'd kept his forbidden book all this time.

Gideon reined Lightning in as they reached the top of the lane. The peddler's wagon lay on its side in the ditch. Later he'd go back and take a good look at it. But first he'd go up and see how the peddler's boy was getting along.

CHAPTER 5

Annie helped Isaac sit up and propped pillows behind him. Then she handed him the bowl.

Isaac poked suspiciously at the meat. "What is this?" he asked in English.

"Why, it's ham," Annie said.

"From a pig?"

"Sure, from a pig!"

Treyf. He handed back the bowl. "Can't eat it," he said.

"How come?"

"Jews don't eat anything that comes from a pig. Ham or bacon or lard."

"Why can't you?" Annie asked. "It's good."

"Can't, that's all." He searched for a way to make her understand. "Pigs are like buttons," he explained. "You don't wear buttons, and I don't eat pig meat. It's a law."

"I see," she said, although the look on her face was doubtful, and she took the soup away.

It had been five days since the Sunday afternoon when Isaac and his father left the brick houses and paved streets of Lancaster behind and headed east along Philadelphia Pike toward the countryside. That first afternoon, every time they passed a handsome black Amish buggy pulled by a fine, fast-stepping horse, Isaac ducked his head in shame and Tateh raised his hand in greeting. The Amish family— father and mother in their dark clothes, the woman's face half hidden by the brim of a black bonnet, the children dressed just like their parents—would wave back. One of them even called out, "Hello, Peddler Jakob!"

"They recognize you!" Isaac said, writhing in embarrassment.

"Not everyone has a horse and wagon like ours," Tateh replied.

Isaac stared at his father with disbelief.

7 1

Tateh seemed actually *proud* of that! "But Tateh, ours looks so . . . so poor compared to theirs," Isaac complained.

"To you, perhaps. To the man who must carry his goods on his back, our wagon is a sign of success, a step up in the world, something to be envied. Everyone must start somewhere, Isaac."

"Maybe so," Isaac admitted grudgingly. But he still turned his face away when a good-looking buggy whirled past them.

By nightfall they had reached the farthest edge of the territory Tateh had sketched on his map, stopping once along the way to eat their kugel. They spread their bedrolls beneath the wagon, protected from the dew. Every bone in Isaac's body ached, especially his behind, which had bounced for miles on the hard wooden seat, but he didn't complain. The stars had come out, and if he lay at a certain angle he could see them winking above him.

Tateh stretched out beside him and locked his hands behind his head. "Now when I was about your age," he began, "your grandfather took me to the annual fair in Ukmergé. He was a dealer in fine furs, the most beautiful sables you can imagine!" Isaac was transported with him back to Russia, their home in the *shtetl,* the visits to the fair. Lying in the darkness, Isaac was still wide awake long after Tateh's voice had fallen silent.

Isaac's first days as a peddler's assistant passed swiftly. Every evening the two made their little "gypsy camp," as Tateh called it, and prepared their feast of boiled eggs and slices of bread thickly spread with fresh pot cheese and scallions, all washed down with cold buttermilk. Sometimes they ate the same thing for breakfast and again at noon. By Wednesday it had begun to seem like less of a feast.

On Thursday Nettie Lapp, one of Tateh's customers, gave them two fat brown cookies wrapped in a bit of paper.

"You know," Tateh said pleasantly in Yiddish, "I do so admire molasses cookies. I think my wife would like to have the recipe, if you would be so kind as to tell it to me."

Nettie Lapp caught some of what he had said. "*Ach,* yes," she said. "But will you remember it?" she asked Isaac in English.

"My assistant will write it down," Tateh said, nodding to Isaac. Isaac got his pencil and paper ready.

"First you soften a cup of lard," Nettie said.

"Fat of a pig," Tateh repeated in Yiddish. Isaac wrote it down, although he already knew he was not going to eat those cookies.

"And then you mix in a cup of molasses and a cup of sour milk, soda in water, and three cups of flour."

"Very good!" Tateh said. "My wife will do well with this, I am certain!"

"What are we going to do with them?" Isaac whispered as they drove off. "They are *treyf.*"

"You will see."

Later, after they had finished their supper, Tateh asked, "Do you still have the *treyf* cookies? Or did you eat them?"

"Stop joking! They are in the wagon."

"Well, get them. We are taking a walk, and we will need them."

They crossed a meadow and made their way through a stand of trees to the bank of a creek, slow-moving and smooth, like polished copper. The sky was turning from rose to lavender.

"Let me have a cookie, if you please." They were still wrapped in paper, which had spots of grease on it. Isaac carried them gingerly, so as not to get the grease on his fingers. Tateh took one and hurled it toward the water with a snap of his wrist. "Now you."

Nettie Lapp's molasses cookie flew high against the pale purple sky and hung there for a moment, like a dark moon, before it fell.

That night, before they spread out their bedrolls and lay down to sleep, Isaac suggested that they open the canvas bag of coins that Tateh carried in the secret pocket of his coat and count the money they had taken in so far, "Just to see."

But Tateh shook his head. "Bad luck,"

he said. "I never count until the week is done and I have brought it home. But," he added with a smile, "I can tell you how much is there, if you really want to know."

"How can you tell without counting?" had asked.

Tateh tapped his head. "I keep it up here. To the penny. Also to the nickel, the dime, and the quarter."

Isaac stared at his father, thinking of the Friday counting ritual. "But you are always surprised when we count it!"

"Not so surprised." He smiled. "It is important that we do that together, you see. Do you still want to know?"

Isaac shook his head.

"And will you keep our secret?"

Isaac nodded.

Isaac remembered the day last winter when he'd come home from school and, finding the house empty, took advantage of this rare chance to creep into the bedroom and lift the lid of the blanket chest. Groping among the layers, he'd found the bulging money stocking and dragged it out. This was the Dream Stocking, the money for the wagon. No one ever said how much money was in this stocking, the money for their future, and Isaac felt he *had* to know.

He'd dumped the money on his cot and started counting. When he heard Mameh's voice, he began furiously scooping the coins back into the stocking, but a stack of pennies scattered in every direction. Isaac plunged the stocking into the chest and frantically crawled around on the floor, collecting pennies. For the next few days he'd seized every opportunity to search under the bed and in the cracks between the floorboards for missing coins, promising himself he'd never do that again.

His resolve lasted barely two weeks before it melted away, and he *had* to get out the money and count it again—just to see it for himself. He was untying the knot when Sarah stepped out from behind the sheet that divided the room.

"Isaac, what are you *doing?*" Sarah was

two years older than Isaac and sometimes sounded uncannily like Mameh.

"Counting the money for the wagon," Isaac confessed. "You were spying on me," he accused.

"Mameh would not like it," Sarah said.

"She will not know if you do not tell her."

"I will keep your secret it you let me count it, too," Sarah bargained, and Isaac gave in.

After that, Sarah and Isaac would count the money in the stocking together, excitedly watching the money grow, sometimes taking reckless chances but never getting caught. Now Isaac wondered if Tateh had known all along what they were doing and let them have their secret, too.

Before sunrise Friday morning—*It was just this morning!*—Tateh had wakened Isaac with a cup of hot, sweet tea. The sky was streaked with red, and the grass around the wagon wore beads of dew. Isaac sipped his tea while his father strapped his tefillin—little leather boxes containing bits of parchment inscribed with scripture—to his arm and forehead, wrapped himself in his prayer shawl, and recited his morning prayers in Hebrew. *This is the last day,* Isaac thought. *The week is almost over.*

The sun still lurked low behind the willow trees when they arrived at their first stop of the day, the Menno Fisher farm. Isaac clambered down from the wagon seat and ran ahead to open the gate. After Goldie and the wagon had passed through, he swung the gate shut and hurried to catch up.

Menno and his sons were already in the field, moving slowly along a furrow with a team of big, heavy-boned horses. Menno's wife, Liza, stopped weeding her flower garden and came to greet them. Tateh introduced Isaac as "my assistant," which made him feel both proud and shy.

Tateh busily opened the wooden boxes to display the inventory. He invited Liza Fisher to feel the quality of the white cloth he offered. "For the husband's shirts," he explained in Yiddish. "Wears like iron." He showed her his royal blue cloth and the bolt of black as well, and finally she chose some of the deep purple. Tateh measured off the amount she wanted, using the distance from his nose to the end of his outstretched arm as a gauge. Next she selected a packet of hooks and eyes and at the last moment held up a pair of scissors. "The best money can buy," Tateh assured her, as she counted out the coins from a leather purse.

When they were finished, Liza Fisher offered them a drink of water from the pump in the yard. Tateh worked the pump handle until a stream of water splashed into the tin cup. They led Goldie to drink from the horse trough. Before they had even reached the county road, Isaac pulled out Mameh's list and with a pencil stub noted the sale.

The plain white farmhouses were set within sight of each other among a patchwork of tender green fields—tobacco mostly, Tateh said, a special kind used to wrap cigars, but also corn and oats and barley, and hay for the dairy cows. Occasionally Tateh passed a farm without stopping. "I went there once," he explained. "They are what the Amish people call 'English.' They do not understand me, and I do not understand them. So I do not go."

"But I could speak to them, Tateh," Isaac said. "I speak English good."

"That is true," Tateh said, turning in at the next lane. "Maybe someday you can teach me to talk English good as you."

At each farmhouse the women and children interrupted their work and gathered eagerly around the wagon as Tateh flipped up the box lids and invited his customers to take a look. Usually the women bought something, and Isaac marked his list.

When the sun stood directly overhead, Tateh judged that it was time to eat. He admired a young mother's chubby new baby and traded her a spool of thread and a cake of shaving soap for a jar of buttermilk, more pot cheese, and another loaf of warm bread. They settled down to eat under a black walnut tree. At least Isaac would not have any more of this for a while—it was Friday, and his next meal would be Mameh's fat Sabbath hen, floating in its own golden broth.

Isaac noticed the puffy white clouds bunching up like sheep. The sun disappeared, a cool breeze sprang up, and the white clouds darkened.

"It cannot always be a day of sunshine," Tateh said. "We will have our oilcloths ready, and I do not think Goldie minds a little rain."

Keeping an eye on the weather, they made another stop. Isaac wished they'd move faster, but Goldie had only one speed—slow. By early afternoon it looked as though it would pour any minute, and as they approached Ezra Stoltzfus's farm, the first drops spattered the dusty road. Isaac jumped down to open the gate, hanging on to his new hat with both hands. Then, the accident.

That was the last thing he remembered before the pain.

Annie was back. She carried a plate with a thick slice of bread spread with pot cheese and sprinkled with scallions and a cup of buttermilk. "How's this?"

"Good," Isaac said and gobbled it up as though it was the most delicious food he had ever tasted.

CHAPTER 6

Gideon found Isaac, bruised and bandaged and asleep on the bed above the hiding place, and Annie sitting by him like a broody hen. Annie gazed up at Gideon with her pretty blue eyes, and Gideon read trouble in them. He guessed without her saying one word: *she's found the clothes.*

"Gideon . . . ," she began, but he shushed her.

"Later," he said.

The boy's eyes fluttered open. He stared at Gideon, glanced in Annie's direction, and then back at Gideon. "Tell her to leave," he whispered urgently in Yiddish.

"What?"

"Tell her to leave," Isaac repeated, this time in English. "I have to . . . to tell you something."

Gideon caught on. "I understand," he said with a wink. "Annie," Gideon said to her, "we need you to go downstairs and get Isaac a drink. Water, maybe, or some buttermilk."

Annie put down her sewing and ran downstairs, her bare feet slapping the wooden steps.

"You got to go, is that it?" Gideon asked.

Isaac nodded.

"Can you walk? As far as the outhouse?"

"I don't know," the boy said in a trembly voice.

"Don't worry," Gideon reassured him. "There's a pot right here."

He pulled a chamber pot out from under the other bed and helped Isaac sit up and hang his legs over the side. Isaac finished using the pot just as Annie's footsteps thumped on the stairs. Isaac pulled his bare legs—he was only wearing one of Datt's shirts—back under the sheet, and Gideon clapped the lid on the pot and handed it to Annie. "Trade you," he said, holding back a smile, and took the cup of buttermilk from her.

Annie's mouth dropped open in a big O. Gideon could see she hadn't thought to offer before. He laughed and said, "Never mind, Annie. I'll take it out." But Annie ran off on her new errand.

He sat down on Annie's chair. "I'm called Gideon," he said.

Isaac swallowed some buttermilk. "Who are the others? There's a little girl who comes and peeks at me and then runs away."

"That's Katie, the youngest. Let's see, you know Mamm by now and Annie, of course. The big man with the red beard is my Datt; folks call him Red Ezra. Amos is my oldest brother—he lives on the next farm down the road. Then comes Levi, then me. Annie's next. Then Ben, he's ten, and Danny's seven, and Katie just turned five. Then Dawdy—Datt's Datt—and Mawmy live in the house next door. Do you have brothers and sisters?"

"Only sisters," Isaac said and told him about Sarah, Tirzah, and Leah. "But we have a new one coming soon. Maybe this week. I hope it's a boy. That's why Tateh had to hurry home, to see about Mameh and the baby."

"And you live in Lancaster City?"

Isaac nodded. "For more than three years now. Before that we lived in New York City. And before that in Russia, where I was born."

"Russia! New York!" Gideon hitched the chair closer and leaned forward eagerly. "You must tell me about those places."

"Sure," Isaac said. "What do you want to know?"

"Everything." Maybe Gideon could ask Isaac some of the questions that he hadn't been able to ask Peddler Jakob. *Besides,* he thought, *the longer the boy talks, the longer I'm away from Datt and his anger. And from Annie and her questions.*

Everything! Isaac hardly knew where to begin. He remembered his life in Russia with fondness but New York City was un-like anything else.

What a place it was! Jews arrived from Eastern Europe, from Russia, by the thousands, by the millions. A river of Jews poured off the ships every day at Ellis Island and joined the flood into the crowded, noisy, dirty city.

The first year in New York had been exciting for Isaac but full of problems. The grammar school in his crowded neighborhood was dark and gloomy as a fortress, and at first he understood almost nothing the teacher said. Like most of the other children he spoke only Yiddish, and the teacher always seemed angry that her pupils didn't speak English. Isaac struggled to learn. There had been no Abie Siegel to tell him what he needed to know.

There had been problems at home, too. Mameh cried constantly, grieving for the dead baby and homesick for the *shtetl*. Tateh looked for work but could find none. He had been a sheepskin trader in Russia, but no one in New York was hiring sheepskin traders. So he became a peddler, carrying a pack loaded with lengths of cloth and needles and thread and other notions. It was a cheap way to start a business—anybody could do it. But it seemed almost every Jew in New York City was trying to make a living as a peddler.

Then Tateh heard from someone, who'd heard it from someone else, about Lancaster County, a rich farming area in Pennsylvania, not too far from New York, where people lived whose ancestors, persecuted for their religious beliefs in Germany and Switzerland and Alsace, had come to America many years earlier. The Amish, as they were called, still clung to their old ways and spoke their old language. "They say the Amish talk is a lot like Yiddish," Tateh had told Mameh from his thirdhand knowledge. "They will make good customers, you will see."

"It is up to you, of course," Mameh said dispiritedly.

Before Isaac's tenth birthday Tateh had gone on ahead to find them a place to live.

At last an envelope arrived containing their train tickets and a slip of paper with a single word in Yiddish: "Come."

Mameh pulled herself out of her melancholy and packed their belongings. Tateh met them at the high-domed railway station and hired a cab to take them to their new home, a narrow two-story brick house with a wooden stoop in front and a real bathtub in the kitchen and the toilet in the basement. Isaac would share one bedroom with his parents, a sheet strung on a clothesline to separate his bed from theirs, and his sisters would sleep in the other. Even Mameh seemed cheered by their new home.

As soon as they were settled, the *mezuzah* with the tiny sacred scroll nailed to the doorjamb, Tateh once more shouldered his peddler's pack and left for the country. All of this led to Isaac being here now.

"But how did you get to New York City from Russia?" Gideon asked.

"On a ship," Isaac said.

"A sailing ship? With a tall mast? Did you see any pirates?"

Isaac studied his companion. Gideon's arms were strong and brown below his rolled-up shirtsleeves. He had eyes as blue as Annie's and a nice smile with even white teeth that glowed in his tanned face. Isaac imagined that his sisters would think Gideon was very handsome, even with his funny haircut. Where had he gotten the idea there were pirates?

"No pirates. And no mast or sails. Just a rusty old steamship with all of us packed into steerage where it stank something terrible and the food was rotten. We were sick most of the time."

Isaac grimaced, remembering the baby who had died on that voyage, and the memory brought to mind the baby about to be born. He hoped God was watching over Mameh. He wondered if Tateh was home yet, and what Mameh had said. *Shabbes* would begin soon. Isaac had never been away from his family on the Sabbath before, and he was beginning to miss his parents and sisters.

"I read a book about pirates," Gideon said in a dreamy way. "*Treasure Island,* by Robert Louis Stevenson. Do you know it?"

"No," Isaac said, shaking loose of his homesickness. He was about to ask Gideon about the pirate book when Annie appeared again in the doorway.

"Mamm says to leave him be, Gideon," she said. "She says he needs to rest so he can get better. She says you should be outside helping Datt and Levi."

"I'm going," Gideon said, standing up. To Isaac he said in a completely different kind of voice, "Soon's you're ready to try to walk, I'll fix you up a crutch." Isaac glanced from Gideon to Annie and guessed from the look on both their faces that something was going on between them.

When Gideon had gone, Annie's mother came up to check on Isaac, gently touching all the places that hurt. They put fresh sheets on his bed, and at Mamm's direction Annie dipped Isaac's cold cloths in springwater one more time and heated up his poultices. Mamm left the chamber pot where he'd be sure to find it. Then they went downstairs, and Isaac was alone.

The rays of the setting sun angled through the panes of the upstairs window and broke into four golden rectangles on the wall above Isaac's bed. Isaac stared at the glowing squares and wondered if Tateh had gotten home yet. He didn't know how long a trip it was on the trolley all the way back to Lancaster, or even when Tateh had left. He could imagine what would happen when his father arrived: Mameh bursting into loud wails as Tateh broke the news of the wrecked wagon, the wounded horse, the ruined merchandise, the injured boy; Tateh, trying to comfort her, explaining that her son was being cared for by gentiles, fed gentile food, sleeping in a gentile bed. Isaac wished he could reassure his mother that he did know *treyf*, that he had refused to eat the pig-fat cookies and pig-meat soup, and that he would continue to be careful not to put anything unclean into his mouth.

At least the canvas bag of coins was safe in the secret pocket of Tateh's coat. Until the wreck it had been a good week, Isaac was certain. Who would be in charge of counting on this Sabbath eve, if Isaac wasn't there? He hoped it would be Sarah.

He thought of his friend Abie. Wouldn't Abie's eyes pop at the stories Isaac would have to tell when he got home! Living with gentiles, eating their food—maybe, before he went home again, he'd eat some of their *treyf* just so he could brag to Abie and agree there was nothing to it. But if Mameh found out, she'd tell Isaac she didn't want him hanging around with a bad boy like Abie.

The golden squares of sunlight moved up the wall, faded, and disappeared. Isaac pictured his mother lighting the candles, and he closed his eyes and prayed along with her: "Blessed art Thou, O Lord our God, King of the Universe..." At home the Sabbath had begun—without him.

Annie sat with Mamm by the coal-oil lamp, mending the boys' pants. Katie had already been put to bed, and Ben and

Danny were catching lightning bugs in the yard. Long after the sun went down, Gideon and Levi and Datt came in from the field. Annie heard their low voices murmuring, the scrape of their boots on the wooden steps, water splashing into the washbowl on the porch while they washed up. That was the signal for Annie and Mamm to cut them each a wedge of shoofly pie, thick with molasses on the bottom and crumbly on top, and to pour them cups of coffee with hot milk, Datt's and Levi's mostly milk, Gideon's almost black. Datt and Levi ate silently.

"How's he doing?" Gideon asked, jerking his head toward the room where Isaac slept. Annie never took her eyes off Gideon, although he wouldn't look at her.

"Better, I think," Mamm said.

"I'm going to make him a crutch. It won't take me but a few minutes."

When Gideon stepped away from the table, wiping his mouth on his sleeve, and went outside carrying a lantern, Annie slipped out after him. He had found a forked branch and leaned it against the fence. "See, all I have to do is smooth this out. Here, Annie, I think you're about the same size he is. Hold this and see if it's the right height." She did as he asked. "Good. Now I just have to whittle this a bit." He glanced up at Annie. "Shouldn't you be going to bed?"

"Gideon, I found the clothes," Annie said in a low voice. In the kitchen Mamm was cleaning up the table. Ben and Danny had gone to the outhouse. "I found the book, too. And the mouth organ." She caught her breath. "What does it mean? Why do you have these forbidden things?"

Gideon frowned and looked away. "I have the book and the mouth organ because I want to read and play music. As for the rest—I can't tell you, Annie. It's better if you don't know."

"But I already know some of it! Gideon, if you don't tell me why you have those clothes and what you're planning to do, I've made up my mind to tell Mamm."

Gideon's sun-bleached eyebrows lifted.

"And if I tell you what you want to know, will you promise not to tell?"

"Yes. I promise."

"You drive a hard bargain, sister."

The screen door creaked open. "Annie?" Mamm called. "You out there?"

"I'm coming!" Annie called. Then she whispered to Gideon, "Meet me in the barn after they're all asleep. Don't forget!" And she ran toward the house.

CHAPTER 7

I'm going to Aaron's up in Big Valley," Gideon explained. "I've been planning it for a long time."

He and Annie huddled in a corner of the barn, near the horses. Maybe it hadn't been such a good idea to come here, Gideon thought; the Stoltzfuses' horses knew Annie and Gideon and paid no attention, but the peddler's horse whinnied.

Gideon couldn't make out Annie's face in the darkness, but he could hear the quaver in her voice. "I don't understand, Gideon. Why must you go anywhere?"

"Because of Datt, mostly," Gideon admitted. "If Levi does something, it's fine; if I do it, it's all wrong. If Amos says something, that's all right; if I say it, I've got the devil in me. And not just that, it's his temper, too. I'm the only son without red hair, and that makes me different. *Dopplig,* that's his favorite word for me."

"But Gideon," Annie reasoned, "if you just tried to talk to him—"

"Annie, don't try to argue me out of it. My mind's made up. Aaron invited me, and I'm going. But," his tone softened, "it doesn't mean I won't miss you and Mamm and everybody."

"But what makes you think you can get along with Datt's brother Aaron when you can't get along with Datt?" Annie demanded.

"I'm just guessing," Gideon admitted. "Aaron treats me different. Maybe it's because I'm his nephew, not his son."

Annie wasn't finished with her questions. "But why do you have *englische* clothes? Don't they dress Amish out where Aaron is?"

Gideon sighed. "That was foolish of me. I guess I was thinking I'd get a job in the city to earn money for my train ticket, and I'd rather do that in *englische* clothes. But I could have just as well have spent that money on the ticket. As for the book and the mouth organ, I have them because I want to read and I want to play music."

"But the *Ordnung* says . . ."

"That's another reason I'm going—to get away from our strict *Ordnung*. Datt's after me to get baptized, but you know that means promising to uphold our *Ordnung*, and I can't. Aaron says they even allow electric lights in the barn out where he is."

"Electric lights!" Annie sounded truly shocked. "Gideon, that's the same as going worldly. Datt says . . ."

"I don't care what Datt says, Annie!"

But before she could argue with him any more, they heard a ruckus in the barnyard. Gideon hurried out to find out what was going on, with Annie on his heels.

"Look," Annie said, "it's Isaac."

Isaac had slept for hours, it seemed, and by the time the Stoltzfus family had retired, he hadn't felt like sleeping any more. Isaac heard the boys murmuring in the room across the hall and the girls in the room next to his. Then it grew quiet. From somewhere beneath him came a rhythmic snoring.

He fidgeted, trying to find a comfortable position, but there was no way to lie that didn't hurt *something*. His mind fidgeted, too. He worried about the wagon, lying wrecked in a ditch. About the unsold merchandise, now mostly ruined. About Goldie, maybe banged up as bad as he was, alone and frightened in the barn. He felt sorry for the poor old thing, even if the crash had mostly been her fault, spooking as she had. Now Tateh would have to buy a new wagon and new merchandise and maybe even a new horse. All this, just when the baby was expected.

How long will I have to stay here? Isaac wondered. Surely Tateh would come back for him before the week was out, before the next Sabbath.

A sliver of moonlight lit the room like a candle. Isaac thought he heard almost silent footsteps in the house, but he might have been wrong. Night sounds flew in through the open window: the insistent cry of the whippoorwill, the hoot of a barn owl, the neigh of a horse. He thought he recognized the horse: *That's Goldie!*

Isaac pushed himself up gingerly with his good arm. His head still ached, but it no longer throbbed as though someone were pounding on it. His feet touched the floor. His shoes were gone. Even worse, his clothes were gone, too, and instead he was dressed in a long white shirt that came halfway to his knees. When he tried to stand up, he discovered that he couldn't put any weight on his left ankle and that his bruised and swollen right hand still wasn't much use. He found the crutch Gideon had left propped beside the bed, hooked it under his good arm, and hobbled cautiously out of the bedroom. In the boys' bedroom someone sighed and muttered, but no one woke up.

Isaac sat down at the top of the steep stairs and slowly eased himself down, step by squeaky step. The crutch got in his way until he reached the bottom and needed it to stand up. The resonant snoring came from behind a door to the left. Isaac hobbled to the right and found himself in the big kitchen. He lurched across the floor toward the table and stumbled against one of the benches, which scraped noisily on the wood floor. He sat down heavily and waited. There was a catch in the snoring, but then it evened out again. After a time Isaac struggled to his feet and continued his journey.

His next destination was the black cast-iron cookstove. Isaac clutched the top to steady himself—it was barely warm—and then tottered toward the back door. The screen door opened with a rusty creak; he took care to close it again as silently as possible. Isaac eased across the porch and, with the help of the banister, hopped on his good right foot down the three steps to the ground.

He stopped to get his bearings. The moon, though only a half, silhouetted the hulking roof of the vast two-story barn and the big barnyard. Between Isaac and the barnyard stretched the garden with row after neat row of vegetables and seed-beds covered with ghostly white cloth. Beyond the garden lay the grassy yard where Rebecca Stoltzfus had strung her clothesline. Isaac recognized his clothes pinned to it and the sheets she'd stripped from his bed and washed by hand. A path edged with whitewashed stones led straight through the center of the garden and the yard, past the clothesline, to the barnyard, which seemed far away.

Suddenly Isaac felt very tired. Goldie would have to wait for daylight and some-one to help him get out to visit her. But then Goldie whinnied again. In that sound Isaac heard a homesickness that echoed his own, and he made up his mind; he would get there on his own.

Isaac began to hop down the path on his good right leg, using the crutch for balance. But he hadn't taken into account the rainstorm that had left the path as slick as grease. Twice Isaac's good foot shot out from under him, and he crashed onto his backside, still sore from the accident. He pulled himself up with the crutch. Even his good leg felt weak. When he reached the garden gate he could see that the barn-yard was a wet and slimy mess. He stopped to rest and catch his breath, took half a dozen steps, fell, and lost the crutch in the mud.

That was the last straw. Isaac decided to turn back. He hoped that Goldie would understand.

Stifling his tears, he struggled to get up, but the more he tried, the more he kept getting tangled up in the long shirt. He managed to crawl on his knees and one good hand back to the gate; he was soaked and dripping with mud. Without the crutch Isaac needed something to hang on to, and he grabbed hold of a pole that happened to be there. But the pole wasn't solidly anchored—it was only a prop wedged under the clothesline to keep it from sagging under the weight of wet wash. When Isaac grabbed the pole, it gave way and the whole thing came down, the sheets and his own damp clothes collapsing on top of him. Isaac howled with pain and frustration. He hadn't cried at all when he got knocked out and banged up—and that had hurt plenty—but this was too much to bear. He lay sobbing on the muddy ground.

Isaac looked up to see Gideon standing over him with a lantern. "You came out to take in Mamm's wash?" Gideon said, lifting the clothesline off him and bracing it with the pole. "She's not going to like what you did to it."

"I was going to visit Goldie," Isaac mumbled, trying not to let Gideon see that he had been crying. "And I fell. I'm sorry I woke you up," Isaac said, so embarrassed he couldn't even look at Gideon.

"You didn't. You want me to carry you back upstairs?"

"No!"

"You'd rather stay out here and let Mamm find you tangled up in her wash? Here, I'll take you piggyback."

Isaac was too exhausted to argue, and it was clear he wasn't able to get there on his own. "All right."

Gideon knelt down so that Isaac could wrap his good arm around Gideon's neck. Then he boosted Isaac onto his back and carried him up to the house just as a light flickered on in the bedroom and Ezra's deep voice boomed, "What's going on out there?"

"We came out to visit Goldie," Gideon hollered back. Isaac saw Annie slip into the house ahead of them, silent as a ghost.

Gideon carried Isaac, muddy and bedraggled, into the kitchen and fetched him a washrag and a basin of water. "I already took care of Goldie's foreleg," Gideon assured Isaac, helping him clean himself up. "Smeared it all over with liniment and bound it up with rags. It'll heal all right, though she's sure not going to win any races for the next couple of weeks. And she may wind up with a limp. Now, if you don't mind, it's time for us both to be in bed."

CHAPTER 8

I t was Saturday, only one day after the wreck, but it seemed to Gideon that Isaac was mending already. The knot on his head had gone down, and it had begun to turn purple. In fact Isaac was turning purple over the better part of his body. His wrist and ankle were still swollen, but the cuts and scrapes were beginning to heal over. *Isaac probably still hurts plenty,* Gideon thought, *but the boy doesn't complain much.*

After he had helped Datt and Levi with the milking, Gideon brought Isaac some pants and a shirt that he'd outgrown. Isaac slipped on the clothes and Gideon helped him hitch up the pants with homemade suspenders.

"You'd look like a real Amishman," Gideon said, studying him, "except for your hair."

He found an old straw hat of Levi's and set it square on Isaac's head. Isaac seemed to hesitate for a moment, but then he tucked his long locks of hair back behind his ears.

"That's better," Gideon said, "but you're still lacking bangs. Now come on down for breakfast."

Datt and the rest of the family were already at the table when Isaac hobbled in, dressed in his borrowed Amish clothes, followed by Gideon. Datt nodded, unsmiling. "I see you're better," he said in English.

"Yes, thank you," Isaac murmured politely.

Ben made room for Isaac on the bench next to Gideon. When they were seated, Datt bowed his head, and everybody stopped for silent prayer. Datt had hardly raised his head and unfolded his hands before Mamm and Annie began setting platters of food on the table. It was a regular

Saturday breakfast: fried mush and molasses, bacon and eggs, fried potatoes. A loaf of bread and a crock of butter were already on the table, along with a pitcher of milk and a pot of coffee.

"Now you just help yourself," Datt said with a glance at Isaac. Datt filled his own plate and passed the platters to Levi. When the food reached Gideon, he loaded up his plate with three sunny-side up eggs, a rasher of bacon, and a slab of mush plus a mound of potatoes on the side. Isaac glanced mournfully at the food and handed it on to Ben.

"Aren't you going to eat anything?" Ben asked.

Isaac stared down at his empty plate. "Can't," he mumbled.

"It's because pigs are like buttons," Annie explained. The food had come around to her side of the table, and she was spooning small servings onto Katie's plate. "We don't put buttons on our clothes, and Jews don't eat meat from a pig. It's in their *Ordnung*." She glanced at Isaac. "Rules," she said. Isaac nodded.

Ben said, "But potatoes aren't pigs. Eggs aren't. Mush isn't."

"I think because they were cooked in lard, which comes from a pig," Annie suggested. "Right, Isaac?"

"Right," he sighed.

"How come he's got a hat on?" Danny piped.

"Another rule," Isaac said, "keeping your head covered. I lost my *yarmulke*."

"Your *what?*" Ben asked.

"It's the skullcap Jewish men and boys always wear."

"You might look like an Amishman," Gideon said, "but you sure don't eat like one."

So Mamm boiled him an egg and sliced some bread for him to dip in the yolk and to spread thickly with pot cheese and apple butter. Isaac put away a good breakfast, although it would not have been enough to satisfy Gideon. When Datt was done, he let out a satisfied belch, and they all bowed their heads for another silent prayer. Then Datt and Gideon and Levi jumped up, ready to head out to the tobacco fields, and Mamm and Annie started clearing the table.

They'd been working these fields since early spring, soon after Datt delivered last year's tobacco to the warehouse. As soon as the ground was thawed, they'd started plowing. Then they prepared the seedbeds next to Mamm's vegetable garden and planted the seeds they'd saved from their best plants last year. Taking care of the seedlings was Annie's job. She kept the seeds covered with cheesecloth while they sprouted, and then she lifted out the tiny seedlings one by one—she had a lot more patience for this kind of work than Gideon had—and set them in shallow wooden boxes. Annie was so proud of those seedlings!

While Datt guided the team up and down the furrows, Levi and Gideon sat on the back of the tobacco planter with the boxes of seedlings. Levi would drop a seedling into a hole poked in the ground and then Gideon would give it a squirt of water and cover it up. They had started planting the first of their eight acres in

May, and now it was June and they were still planting. The first crop would be cut in August; the seedlings they were putting in now wouldn't be ready for cutting until September.

At the end of each day they'd take the empty boxes back to Annie, and she'd have others ready for the next day. But since Isaac came yesterday, she'd fallen behind. Ben and Danny had tried to prepare some boxes, but they were clumsy and slow. There were a few ready, but not enough for a full day's work in the field.

"All right," Datt said around midmorning. "No more planting today. I have some errands in town. Levi, you come with me." He scratched his chin under his red beard. "Here's what you do, Gideon: go take a look at the peddler's wagon and figure what it needs to fix it up. All next week we'll have our hands full, getting ready for the preaching. Maybe we can find time to work on the wagon when that's over."

Gideon found Isaac sitting on the

porch, playing with Katie's kitten. "I'm going to look at the wagon," Gideon said. "You want to come along and tell me what you think? I'll carry you piggy-back."

"I can walk," Isaac insisted.

Gideon shrugged. Isaac plainly had a hard time getting around, even with the crutch Gideon had rescued from the barnyard and cleaned up for him, but he couldn't admit it. "Suit yourself," Gideon said.

"You could take the wheelbarrow," Annie suggested, coming out of the kitchen where she was helping Mamm with the baking for the company expected on Sunday. "And hunt for things to salvage. Then if Isaac gets tired, he can ride."

"Good idea, Annie," Gideon said.

But Isaac objected. "I can't," he said. "It's the Sabbath. We're not allowed to ride anywhere on the Sabbath."

"What if I carry you?" Gideon asked. "Wouldn't that be permitted for somebody who's hurt?"

"All right," Isaac agreed finally. "But only if I can't go any farther on my own."

Ben and Danny naturally wanted to come, too. They ran to ask Datt, who had other plans for them—cleaning the chicken coop—but he relented. "Clean it when you come back," he said. "Mind you don't forget."

The boys didn't wait for him to change his mind. Then Mamm told Annie she should go, too, and suggested packing a lunch. It was turning into a holiday, Gideon thought, something rare for this time of year when the family was too busy to take time off for picnics.

Mamm padded the wooden wheelbarrow with old feather pillows and spread a worn-out quilt over them, just in case. She pinned up Isaac's arm in a sling ripped from an old bedsheet, so he would not be tempted to use it too soon, and warned him, "Now don't overdo. You're still mending. Annie," she said, "you watch out for him. Go slow."

It was amazing, what all they found as

they retraced Goldie's path before the wagon had rolled over: clothesline rope unraveled from its bundles, clothespins scattered every which way, washboards of rippled galvanized tin, and a couple of flatirons that had landed in the bushes. They fished a bolt of blue cloth, still wrapped around a wooden board, out of the ditchwater. A bolt of purple cloth had come unwound and hung twisted along the fence. Several pairs of scissors and a couple of pocketknives glinted in the tall grass. They gathered up green-painted darning eggs that had nearly disappeared in the weeds. Although he didn't find Isaac's new peddler hat, sharp-eyed Ben spotted a little black cap near the gate, wet and covered with mud. They collected whatever they found in old feed sacks and brought the dirty, soggy stuff to Isaac, who'd managed to hobble the whole way. Now he rested in the wheelbarrow and watched them.

"My *yarmulke!*" Isaac exclaimed and clapped the muddy skullcap on his head under the straw hat. "I wish I could help," he said. "But we're not allowed to work on the Sabbath."

"That's all right," Gideon assured him. "There are plenty of us to do it."

While Annie and Ben and Danny poked through the tall grass, Gideon inspected the wagon. At first he thought it was a total loss, but the more he studied it, the more he saw possibilities for fixing it up. They'd have to get several men to lift it out of the ditch and heave it up on a hay wagon to move it back to the barn. The two wheels that had come off were both damaged, and the two still on the wagon looked to be bent here and there, but a wheelwright could repair them. The axletree was ruined, and the shafts to which Goldie had been harnessed were nothing but splinters. Gideon added new sideboards to the list, and at least two new boxes and a couple more lids, and while they were at it, a new seat, although the split and warped old one had somehow got through the wreck in one piece. *That one looks hard on the backside,* Gideon thought. A few other little things and it would be good as new. *Better* than new. Better than poor old Goldie deserved. She'd look sorrier than ever pulling this wagon when Gideon got done with it.

Annie came to fetch him. "I thought you'd be hungry by now."

"I'm always hungry," Gideon admitted and followed her back to the meadow.

Annie was wearing a dark blue dress, and she had rolled the long sleeves almost to her elbows. The triangular shawl over her shoulders was carefully pinned in front and back to her apron. Her apron was pinned, too, because tying strings in a bow was not allowed. Thoughts of the forbidden bow caused Gideon's mind to skip to the necktie he had recently bought and added to his hoard of forbidden clothes; he still had no idea how to tie it, and he wondered how he'd learn before it was time to leave.

Looking at Annie's white cap, her slim back, her tough bare feet flashing below the hem of her long, full skirt, Gideon felt a rush of tenderness for his sister. Annie was so pretty, and so smart and nice, too. In another year or so the young men would come courting, inviting her for spins in their bachelor buggies, taking her home from the Sunday night singings and the Saturday night frolics. He wondered who she'd end up with and mentally checked off some of the boys her age and older. One of his friends, maybe? That brought to mind that he had told Lizzie Esh he'd take her home from the singing a week from Sunday. Lizzie was good and a hard worker, too, and almost as pretty as Annie. He let his thoughts linger on Lizzie.

On days like this Gideon thought he'd be a fool ever to leave. If he stuck it out and did what was expected of him, followed the rules, got baptized like Datt wanted, he'd have a place of his own someday, and a good wife—if not Lizzie Esh, then somebody like her—and a whole slew of little dishwashers and woodchoppers growing up around him. A man couldn't ask for a better life than farming or a prettier place to be than right here. As long as he obeyed the rules.

But that's what got him down: the *Ordnung*. There was a rule for every little thing, from the width of your hat brim to the length of your hair and whether you could have a whipsocket on your buggy or a bit of metal trim on your harness and whether you could own a worldly book. Everything depended on your church district. And it wasn't as if you could choose which church district you wanted; you belonged where your family belonged, unless you were like Aaron and willing to pay the price of being shunned.

Gideon hadn't looked at *Treasure Island* in a long time. If Datt ever found the book, he would rip the pages out and burn them. Then would come the smacking with the buggy whip. Gideon wouldn't miss any of that. But he sure would miss Annie.

Annie and Ben and Danny had collected a number of sodden paper packets of pins and needles plus a few muddy envelopes of hooks and eyes. They'd also found dozens of spools of thread in several colors, but mostly black and white and all very dirty, and a tin box of thimbles, shut tight with not a single one missing. But their prize discovery so far was Isaac's bedroll with a set of his clothes inside, wrapped in oilcloth and tied with twine.

"We'll look some more after we eat," Ben said. "I'm hungry."

"We could put stuff in the basket if we eat the lunch now," Danny suggested. He was very practical for a seven-year-old.

Annie unpacked the bread-and-butter sandwiches and half-moon pies Mamm had sent along and laid them out on a clean dish towel. There were two apiece.

Isaac picked up one of the pies. "What's in this?"

"Schnitz," Ben said. "If you cut an apple in half, you get halves. If you cut it again, you get quarters. If you cut it again, eighths, and then sixteenths. But if you cut it still again, you get *schnitz.* That's what Teacher taught us. Then you dry them and keep them for making pies. We've got baskets and baskets of *schnitz* in our cellar."

Isaac broke open his little pie, and thick, gooey apple and cinnamon oozed out. He took one bite and stopped.

"What's in the pastry? I mean, what's it made with?"

"Oops," Annie said. "Fat of a pig. I forgot."

He spit the bite of pie onto the ground and handed his half-moon pies to Ben and Danny. "You can have them," he said. "There's only one bite missing." Danny didn't seem to care about the missing bite. Gideon passed his extra bread-and-butter sandwich to Isaac, thinking, *He sure is good about sticking to the rules. Better than I'd be.*

When Ben and Danny had run off to make another search of the area and Isaac had dozed off in his nest in the wheelbarrow, Annie said, "Show me the wagon, Gideon."

They climbed over the ditch and Gideon pointed out what he thought was needed to put the wagon back in shape. "If we get Reuben Beiler and John Lapp and some others to help out, it won't take but a day."

Annie quit studying the wagon and turned to look at him with the scared and worried look he'd seen on her face so often the past few days. *"When,* Gideon? You didn't say when you're going."

"Soon."

"Promise you won't just up and leave without telling me," she said. "Promise you'll tell me when you plan to go."

"Annie, you're making it so hard for me . . ."

Her jaw jutted out. "I know! I want to make it hard, Gideon! I want to make it impossible, if I can!"

Annie has changed, Gideon thought. She never used to be so stubborn, so determined. What was happening to his sweet little sister who never argued with him?

He put his hands on her shoulders. "If I promise to tell you when I'm going, will you promise not to try to stop me?"

She gazed at him with tears gathering in her blue eyes. "No," she said finally. "I can't promise that."

"Don't worry, Annie," he said. "You'll know. Now let's go home and clean out the chicken coop before Datt gets back."

CHAPTER 9

Mamm had Annie and the boys spread out the goods they had salvaged on the kitchen table and the wooden benches. The boys went out to clean the chicken coop, and Mamm began sorting the goods into piles: "This is all right. This can be fixed. This maybe can be fixed. But this looks bad—we'll see." The first pile was very small; the last, hopeless pile, a little larger. Annie saw that everything else needed work.

The pocketknives and scissors, Mamm decided, called for polishing, first with a rough cloth and then a soft one. She used a pair of these scissors to cut the length of purple cloth into pieces, snipping out the parts that were torn but saving even these odds and ends for her scrap bag. "We'll wash it good," she said, holding up one of the longer pieces. "It won't fetch a high price, but someone can use it."

Annie took the needles out of the soggy paper packets and stuck them in rows in a clean square of paper cut from an old newspaper. Isaac told her how to make orderly rows, the longest needles with the biggest eyes in the center of the square, the small, fine needles tapering down on either side. When she'd finished the needles, she started on the straight pins.

"I can help after sundown," Isaac said, "when Sabbath is over."

"No need," Annie said. "It goes quick."

By the time the boys came in from their chore, Annie was threading together a series of hooks and eyes.

"How come," Isaac asked, "you don't use buttons?"

"Buttons are worldly," Mamm said.

"But what does worldly mean?"

"Why, it means in the way of this world we're living in now. We believe it's our duty to keep ourselves separate from this evil world. Our people have used hooks and eyes since before the first Amish people came from across. Hooks and eyes aren't worldly."

"Does it say that in the Bible?"

"Something like it," Mamm said.

" 'Be ye not conformed to this world,' " Gideon quoted, pouring himself a cup of buttermilk, " 'but be ye transformed by the renewing of your mind that ye may prove what is that good and acceptable and perfect will of God.' That's Romans, twelfth chapter. Besides, soldiers' uniforms in Germany always had rows and rows of buttons, and Amish don't believe in war or in serving in the army."

Annie stared at her brother in amazement. She had never heard him quote from the Bible before.

"Tateh says lots of Jews left Russia because they didn't want to fight in the czar's army. They weren't allowed to observe the Sabbath, and they couldn't get kosher food. The kind of food we can eat," Isaac added.

"Isaac won't eat *schnitz* pies," Ben said. "The ones in our lunch. He gave them to us."

"Because of the lard," Isaac explained.

"*Ach*, I forgot!" Mamm exclaimed. "Next time, I'll remember."

"What's the matter with lard?" Danny asked.

"It's *treyf*," Isaac said.

"*Treyf?*" It was Ben's turn to question.

"The opposite of kosher," Isaac said.

"*Whssssht*, you ask too many questions," Mamm told Ben and Danny, but Annie was sorry the discussion had come to an end.

Late in the afternoon Mamm selected three plump hens to be prepared for the company who would come on Visiting Sunday and lopped off their heads on a stump near the chicken coop with three swift strokes of her cleaver. Annie's job was plucking their feathers, a chore she hated. Saturday night supper was a simple meal: fried scrapple and creamed lettuce from Mamm's garden. When scrapple was explained to him—scraps of pork mixed with cornmeal—Isaac made a face and reached for the crock of pickled red beets and eggs. Annie watched him bite into the hard-boiled egg that had been pickled with the beets and had soaked up their purplish color and the sour vinegar taste all the way through to the yolk. Silently she passed him the bowl of pot cheese with an extra layer of cream floating on top and a dish of apple butter.

Nobody talked much at supper, as usual. Datt asked Gideon if he had looked at the peddler's wagon, and Gideon said he had and described what he thought needed to be done.

"Levi, you take a look Monday and see what you think," Datt said, and Annie saw Gideon try to hide his disappointment and anger. Why couldn't Datt just take Gideon's word for it? "Can't get to it next week, what with the preaching here next Sunday. Say the week after. Make it Tuesday a week," Datt continued.

Isaac's head popped up. "A week from Tuesday?" he asked in English. He seemed to pick up about half of whatever they said in Dutch. "Not until then?"

"That's right." Datt turned to Mamm. "It'll be another meal for you," he said. "We'll have ten or twelve here to help."

"No trouble," Mamm said, although Annie knew it would be a lot of trouble for everybody.

By Saturday evening the work week was over, and except for feeding the animals and the milking, it was a time to rest. Mamm and Annie stitched on their quilts. Datt read *The Budget,* the weekly newspaper that carried news of Amish settlements clear across Pennsylvania and all the way out to Iowa. Annie wondered if he ever found news of his brother Aaron. Datt would never say if he did, though. Annie felt a stab of pain when she realized that someday she might be searching for news of Gideon in that paper. She bent closer to the patches she was sewing.

Ben set up a checkerboard on the kitchen table and challenged Danny to a game, the winner to play Isaac. Katie dressed and undressed the rag doll Mawmy had made her. Its tiny outfit matched Katie's, but the doll had no features on its plain muslin face, as the *Ordnung* required.

Levi had gone out. Nobody said a word when he'd polished his buggy, bathed in the washhouse and changed into his good clothes, and came in to announce that he was taking a little drive down the road to give Robin some exercise.

He acted like nobody knew he was courting Nancy Esh, and of course everybody went along with it. That's the way Amish courtships were carried on: in secret, with the family pretending it had no idea what the young man was up to. But for over a year Levi had been going to see Nancy every other week, on the Saturday night before Visiting Sunday, the off-Sunday when there was no preaching. Annie found out about the courtship when Lizzie Esh told her she'd gotten up to visit the outhouse and had seen Levi sneaking out of their house one night long after the parents were asleep. Annie guessed that Lizzie would give a lot to have Gideon courting her, judging from the way Lizzie smiled at him.

Annie stitched on her quilt and out of the corner of her eye watched Gideon, who stared moodily out the window. She wished he'd go out courting, too. Datt would approve if Gideon ended up married to Lizzie, because Nancy's and Lizzie's father, Joseph Esh, was a deacon in their church. Joseph's hat brim was wider than anybody's except Grossdawdy's. But Gideon did not seem to be going anywhere.

Danny managed to beat Ben at checkers, Isaac beat Danny easily, and then Ben wanted a chance to play Isaac, too. Annie went over to watch them for a while before Datt finished his paper and, yawning, announced that he was going to bed, and everyone else must, too.

Annie generally enjoyed Visiting Sunday, when there was no long preaching to sit through. Sometimes Datt hitched up the buggy and took the family to call on friends. And sometimes it happened that everybody got the notion to go visiting at the same time; you could go to three or four different farms before you found a family at home.

This Sunday Datt decided that the family would stay at home. After the milking and other chores were done, Mamm sent Gideon to tell Amos and Barbara to be sure and come over with little Davy, who was barely three months old. The three chickens were stewing, and Annie was mixing the dumpling dough to drop in the bubbling broth. When Isaac asked what was in the dish, Annie explained that the gravy was made with milk and the dumplings with butter, and that was the end of it for him.

"Milk and meat together is forbidden," he told Annie. "Like lard."

"So why don't you just eat the chicken?" Annie asked impatiently. She was hanging a clean towel on the roller above the washbasin on the porch.

"There's another thing," Isaac said. "Your Mamm killed the chickens herself. You don't have a *shochet,* a ritual slaughterer, to make sure the animals are killed the right way, with a special knife sharpened in a particular way, so the meat is clean. Before we moved out here from New York, Mameh made sure there was a Jewish butcher with a *shochet* in Lancaster."

"You better not tell Mamm her meat isn't clean," Annie warned him. "She won't like that one bit."

Mawmy and Grossdawdy always arrived first, since they lived right next door. Around eleven o'clock Mamm's sister Lena and her husband, Abner, and their kids drove up, followed by their neighbors Reuben and Amelia Beiler with their three daughters. Amos and Barbara showed up with Davy, just as Mamm was lifting the dinner, putting the food in serving dishes.

Annie hustled around the kitchen with the other women, setting out the bowls and heaping platters, and then Mamm called the men to the table. Annie stood ready to refill the serving dishes as they were emptied. She smiled when she saw Isaac take a place next to Ben and wait until the silent prayer had ended. He filled his plate with his usual pot cheese and apple butter, pickled red beets and eggs.

She thought of Isaac sitting out on the porch early this morning, trying to whistle. He said his Tateh was a great whistler, and Isaac wanted to be like him. But Datt heard him. "No whistling on Sunday," Datt had said in his stern way, and Isaac quit and clamped his lips shut.

"How come I can't whistle on Sunday?" he'd asked Annie later.

"Because it's the Sabbath," she said quietly.

After the men finished eating, the women took their places. It was pouring down rain again, so when dinner was over the younger children went out to the barn to play and the sitting room filled up with adults. Mawmy and the other grand-mothers puffed on their pipes—only the old women smoked—and talked about their grandchildren and about how to get rid of cutworms in the cucumbers. The men discussed plans for cutting alfalfa, and they decided who could come to fix the wrecked wagon. And Annie waited for a chance to talk to Barbara alone.

Katie made faces at the baby to keep him entertained, and Barbara began asking Isaac questions about his family. Annie saw Datt frown. He didn't approve of this type of idle conversation. And he never did take to Amos's wife, Annie knew, because of her father. In addition, Datt believed Barbara was too forward. Annie could see that he was getting more and more irritated.

"Why don't you take your women's gossip out to the kitchen?" Datt interrupted. Barbara stopped in the middle of a sentence. Abruptly she scooped up Davy and ran upstairs. Annie followed her.

"Don't mind Datt," Annie whispered. "You know how he gets."

"Sure, I know how he gets," Barbara said. She sat down on one of the beds in the spare room, preparing to nurse the baby. Annie sat beside her, admiring Davy's delicate fringe of reddish hair. From this angle Annie could see where the hidey-hole was, beneath Isaac's bed.

Annie had been hungering for this opportunity, but now that she had it, she wasn't sure what to say. She had made a solemn promise to Gideon not to tell Mamm, and Datt was included in that promise. But she had not specifically promised not to tell Barbara. She took a deep breath.

"Barbara," she whispered. "Gideon's got *englische* clothes. You can even see from here where he's hidden them, in a space under that bed. I found them by accident."

Barbara smiled. "Lots of boys do that. I always thought it would be fun to do that myself—put on a worldly dress and go to the city. I never did, of course," she added quickly, "but I wouldn't be too surprised if Amos did something like that."

Annie looked at her, stunned. "But Amos didn't leave," Annie stammered. "He stayed and married you! Gideon is planning to go away."

"He is? How do you know?"

But before Annie could pour out the whole story, Mamm came to the foot of the stairs and called up softly, "Annie? I need you to come and pass cookies to our guests."

Annie sighed and went downstairs to help. Then Annie's friend, Lila Beiler, called her out to the barn and they got to botching, a hand-slapping game. Around four o'clock everyone went home to milk and do the chores. The chance to talk to Barbara had slipped away.

CHAPTER 10

Before breakfast on Monday, Gideon built a fire in the stove in the washhouse and filled the washtub for Mamm. Annie helped her mother put the wash into the tub, a batch at a time: first the bedsheets, which had to be boiled to get them white; next, the family's underclothes; then the white dress shirts. Annie turned the crank on the wringer, and Mamm fed the wet clothes through the rollers to the rinse water.

Between the white wash and the colored wash, Mamm took the lengths of cloth salvaged from the peddler's inventory and sloshed them around with a wooden pole until she judged them clean. They added more water to the tub as it was needed and more of the yellow lye soap they'd made after the fall butchering. Then they washed their aprons and dresses and, last, the men's work shirts and britches.

Mamm and Annie worked all day, lugging baskets of wet wash out to the yard to hang on the clothesline. A stiff breeze dried things quickly. By the time Annie was pinning the trousers and shirts to the line, the lengths of cloth were dry and ready to be taken in.

On Tuesday after the men left for the fields and Isaac had gone out to the barn to visit Goldie, Mamm laid two wooden planks across the backs of a pair of straight chairs and padded the planks with a blanket and an old bedsheet. Then she heated a couple of flatirons on the cookstove, tested one with a spit-dampened finger, and began to press Datt's shirts. When one iron cooled, the other was hot and ready to use. When Mamm stopped to fix dinner, Annie worked on aprons and britches.

It was the middle of the afternoon

when they began to work on the cloth from the peddler's wagon. As Mamm finished each piece, Annie measured it with a wooden yardstick and marked the measurement—so many feet, so many inches—on a scrap of paper, folded the cloth, and pinned the paper to it. Pretty soon almost the entire contents of Peddler Jakob's wagon had been cleaned up, fixed up, and laid out on a table in the sitting room. Not much had to be thrown away after all. Even the muddy wooden spools of thread had been unwound, washed, dried, and rewound, although not the perfect way it had been done in the factory. The peddler would be pleased and grateful, Annie was sure. He would be pleased and grateful about his son, too. Isaac was improving each day, although he still limped a little when he walked, and his bruises had faded to a stormy shade of purple and green. Goldie was improving, too. Isaac had taken over the chore of feeding and watering her twice a day, and Gideon had showed him how to check the dressings on her injured leg.

But Annie felt sorry for Isaac. She noticed that Isaac had taken to hobbling out to the gate a couple of times a day, always returning with a disappointed expression. *It must be hard to be away from home,* Annie thought. *Especially when you're hurting all over and have to stay among strangers.*

"He said he'd come back in a week, Isaac," Annie reminded him. "It's only been four days."

"I know."

Then it was five days. Then six.

Thursday was the day they began getting the house ready for the preaching, and Annie had no time to think about Peddler Jakob.

Datt and Levi and Gideon took down the removable partitions between the downstairs rooms and carried the furniture from the sitting room and Datt's and Mamm's bedroom out to a shed to make room for the benches. They would be delivered on Saturday, unloaded from the wagon, and arranged in rows in the downstairs rooms. Datt and Mamm would sleep upstairs in the spare room for a few nights, so Isaac had to be moved out of the spare room and into the big bedroom with Levi, Gideon, Ben, and Danny.

Annie, Mamm, and Mamm's sister Lena took up the big rag rugs and draped them over the fence and thumped them with wire carpet beaters. While the rugs were up, they scrubbed and waxed all the floors downstairs. There were no curtains, but the windows had to be washed inside and out. Mawmy took over some of the light chores like washing Mamm's pretty china serving dishes, which would be used for the noon meal. Mamm gave Annie the job of blackening the cookstove and the stove in the sitting room.

Not only did the inside of the house need to be made ready but the outside, too—the yard tidied, the trunks of the trees whitewashed, the flower beds fixed just so. Datt and Levi and Gideon shoveled out the stables and spread clean straw over the manure pile and whitewashed the lower part of the barn.

On Friday morning Amos came over

to help out and brought Barbara and the baby along. *Maybe I can talk to her more about Gideon,* Annie thought, *when she's got a minute extra.* But then several neighbor women arrived to help with the baking in the outdoor oven: at least forty *schnitz* pies, twenty loaves of bread, and twenty dozen cookies to pass around to the children during the long service. Others tended kettles of bean soup on the cookstove. Davy was put to sleep in a basket upstairs in the spare room, with Katie in charge of watching over him. Barbara seemed to have no extra minutes.

But later, when Barbara did sit down to rest for a bit, she called to Annie, "Where's Isaac?"

"Whitewashing the outhouse," Annie said.

"I almost forgot. We brought up the mail, and there's a letter for him. I put it on the kitchen shelf. Would you see he gets it? He's probably anxious." Her voice dropped to a whisper. "We'll talk later, Annie. About Gideon." She squeezed Annie's hand.

Annie reached up to the shelf where

Datt kept his German Bible. Next to it was the latest edition of *The Budget,* a letter from Mamm's cousin up near Ephrata, and a letter addressed to Isaac Litsky, in care of Ezra Stoltzfus, R.F.D. Intercourse. It was postmarked Lancaster.

She found Isaac with a bucket and a broad brush, a good part of him spattered with whitewash. "Isaac!" she called, hurrying down the path. "Here's a letter for you!"

Isaac studied the envelope, addressed to him in Sarah's angled script. He wiped his hands on his pants and carefully tore it open. Sarah had written to him in Yiddish. That made him more homesick than ever.

"Dear Isaac," she wrote, "I am writing to tell you that we have a new baby brother. He was born last evening, Tuesday. He is fine and healthy, thank G-d, but Mameh is very weak and tired and must stay in bed. Tateh has asked me to write that he will come for you as soon as Mameh has regained some of her strength. We are all worried about you and hope that your injuries are healing. We will be happy when you come home again. Your loving sister, Sarah."

Isaac tried to digest the news that Tateh would not be coming for him today, and again he would miss being home for the Sabbath. He folded the letter back in the envelope. "It's from my sister Sarah," he explained to Annie, who had been inspecting his whitewash job. "I have a new baby brother. Tateh isn't coming for another week because Mameh is still in bed." Isaac struggled to hide his disappointment about the delay.

"That's mostly good news, isn't it? The baby is fine, and you can stay here as long as you want to. By the time your Datt comes, they'll have the wagon fixed up good as new," Annie said. "That will be a good surprise for him, I think. And we like you being here."

Isaac didn't know how to say what he felt. Except for the food, and for being away from home on the Sabbath, he didn't mind being there. But there was something else he couldn't quite put his finger on. He sensed trouble in this family. Rebecca Stoltzfus was kind and gentle; she reminded Isaac of his own dear Mameh. He liked Annie a lot, and Gideon and the others, too. But Ezra Stoltzfus was a stern man with fierce gray eyes, and he seemed to be angry about something.

The family didn't talk much at the table—not like the lively meals at his own home! And when they did talk, Isaac could follow only part of what they said, unless they spoke English for his benefit. But even without knowing the language he could sense a difference in the way Ezra spoke to Gideon and the way he spoke to the rest of the family. And Gideon seemed completely different when his father was around. Something, Isaac concluded, was going on between Ezra and Gideon. Whatever it was made Isaac uncomfortable, even though he knew it had nothing to do with him.

"I've never been away from my family before," he explained to Annie. "It's nice here, but do I miss them. Our Sabbath begins at sundown today, and that makes me miss them even more."

"I've never been away from home, either," Annie said. "I don't think I ever want to be away from my people. At least not for very long."

"It's hard," Isaac admitted. "I remember when we left the village where I was born. My grandmother cried and cried. She said she'd never see us again, and it was like we were dying. Mameh cried, too. It was very sad."

"Did you ever see her again?" Annie asked.

"No. I don't think we will, either." Isaac picked up the brush dripping with the mixture of lime and water and went back to whitewashing the outhouse. "Once you leave, you don't go back."

"Oh," he heard Annie say. She sounded strange.

Isaac turned around. She looked strange, too. "What's wrong, Annie?"

"It's Gideon," Annie said. "He's planning to leave." She poured out the story. "Maybe you can help, Isaac," she said, twisting her apron. "Help me think of a way to stop him."

But she ran away before Isaac could tell her that he thought it might be a good idea for Gideon to leave, after all.

CHAPTER **11**

B_y Saturday the house was turned completely upside down, and every room downstairs was crowded with rows of backless benches. Every time Isaac looked for Annie, she was scrubbing something. He had never seen such a housecleaning in his life. Even Mameh's preparation for Passover was nothing like this.

The memory brought on another attack of homesickness. Before Passover every spring Mameh worked feverishly to rid their home of every speck of *chametz*— any kind of grain or leavened bread, forbidden during the Passover season. She was relentless in her search for stray crumbs, which she collected with a feather and threw into the fire. Tateh,

Mameh said, was the worst offender with pretzel crumbs that showed up in the pockets of his coat. When every crumb had been destroyed, the regular dishes were put away and the special Passover dishes brought out: one set for *milkhik,* dairy, and another for *fleyshik,* meat.

And the food! There was lots and lots of it: gefilte fish, and Isaac's favorite, *tsimmes*—brisket cooked until it was falling apart with prunes and sweet potatoes in the rich broth—and Mameh's special sponge cake made with matzo meal.

The cooking smells in this gentile house were strange to Isaac, not at all like the smells from Mameh's kitchen, and he didn't like them. He wondered if Abie Siegel was telling the truth about eating frankfurters and ham sandwiches at the market; how could he do it without gagging? Annie's family tried hard to make him feel at home, but he was sure he would never eat another purple egg as long as he lived.

On Thursday night, Isaac had been moved into the bedroom with the Stoltzfus boys, and Gideon had crawled in with Ben and Danny so that Isaac could have his bed. Now, on Saturday night, a scuffle broke out in the bed with the three boys in it, until Levi shushed them. At last everything grew quiet, but still Isaac couldn't sleep.

He felt for the letter from Sarah under his pillow, the first letter he had ever received. At home his family had bid farewell to Queen Sabbath, and Isaac had missed all of it. He thought of Mameh and Tateh and the new baby, and of his three sisters, and he yearned to be with them. All he could do was recite the prayer Mameh always said, but it was not at all the same. Tomorrow would be the Sabbath in this Amish household. Isaac hoped that God would forgive him if this one time he observed someone else's Sabbath instead of his own.

Isaac crawled sleepily out of bed on Sunday morning. The sun was not up yet, but the family was already busy with the chores. The horses and chickens and pigs had to be fed and the cows milked. As usual, Isaac fed Goldie and assured her that everything was all right. Once the chores were done, everyone hurried to wash up at the basin on the porch and dress for the preaching—whatever *that* was.

Isaac asked Ben, who explained, "Why, it's *preaching*, mostly. There's hymns and prayers and such, and the minister talks for a long, long time. Dawdy is one of the preachers. You'll begin to wish you were someplace else!"

"I'm not going," Isaac mumbled.

"Not going?"

"I'm Jewish," Isaac reminded Ben. "It's not right for me to go."

"Oh. Well. Better tell that to Datt. He's real strict about it," Ben said.

But Ezra Stoltzfus seemed to have so much else on his mind that Isaac was sure he wouldn't be missed if he wasn't there.

They were finishing up a hurried breakfast of crumb cake dunked in coffee and hot milk—"The cake is made with butter, Isaac," Rebecca remembered to tell him—when the grandparents walked in from next door. Just then a long line of open bachelor buggies and gray-topped family buggies began rolling up the lane. Ezra went out to welcome them, dressed in a long black tailcoat with a vest under it and the wide-brimmed black hat his wife had just finished brushing. His great red beard flowed down the front of his broad chest. Levi and Gideon were also dressed in black coats, their black hats brushed, their black shoes polished. Even Ben and Danny had on sober black suits.

Rebecca Stoltzfus wore a dark green dress with a matching shawl and apron and a white cap. But the shawl and apron over Annie's deep purple dress were white, and she had put on a black cap instead of her everyday white one. Katie's clothes were exactly like Annie's, even to her little cap.

Ezra greeted each man and his family as they arrived in the barnyard. When the passengers had alighted, Gideon and Levi drove the buggies to the pasture and hitched the horses to the fence rail. Ben and Danny ran back and forth, feeding the horses hay. The bearded men and beardless boys gathered near the barn, the women in white caps and girls in black caps by the washhouse.

Isaac kept off by himself, feeling strange and out of place. He'd dressed in his own clothes, the ones that had been packed in the bedroll, and he'd borrowed Gideon's hat. People glanced at him curiously and nodded but then looked away. *It's the payess,* Isaac thought, *that's why they're staring.* He tucked his earlocks out of sight, thinking of Abie Siegel as he did.

"Soon as I'm thirteen, I'm going to cut off my *payess,*" Abie had told him. "Whack, whack, like that. You should, too. You look like you're just off the boat."

"No!" Isaac protested. "We can't, Abie. The earlocks are a symbol." He couldn't remember exactly what the *payess* symbolized—but he would never forget his grandfather's anguish when the Russians cut his off.

"Symbol of being a foreigner, that's

what," Abie had snorted. "If you want to look like a real American, Isaac, you got to get rid of the *payess*. This here isn't the *shtetl*."

Isaac didn't think he could do it. It wasn't like eating *treyf,* which was private, something only he would know he had done. It would be like one of the boys wearing "English clothes," as Annie called them: everyone would know. Isaac wanted to be a real American, not a foreigner. But he wanted to be a Jew, too. Abie made it sound as though you couldn't be both. He hoped Abie was wrong.

People began lining up outside the house, women in one line, men in another. Old white-bearded men were first, and the youngest boys, including Ben and Danny Stoltzfus, came last. "You're lucky," Ben whispered to Isaac as he hurried to get in place. "I wish I could stay out here with you." Then the solemn procession filed silently into the farmhouse, and Isaac was left alone.

Curious, Isaac crept close to a window and peered in. Soon the benches were filled, men and boys on one side of the room, women and girls on the other. The men swept off their hats all at the same time and set them on the floor, and an old man with a long white beard in the front row started singing in a high, nasal voice. Everybody joined in the slow, wailing chant. It seemed to go on and on, but when it stopped, Annie's grandfather stood up and began to speak in a deep, gentle singsong. Isaac couldn't understand what he was saying, and he soon got bored and wandered away.

First Isaac went to look over the buggies parked in a long, even row in the pasture—he counted thirty of them. He walked from horse to horse, stroking their long, graceful necks, patting their sleek sides and thick manes. Poor Goldie had probably never been as pretty as any of these horses, even when she was young.

Isaac tramped back to the barnyard, stopping at the chicken coop and sending the hens squawking and huffing off in a flurry of feathers. A couple of geese honked at him and waddled away. He inspected the corncrib where ears of dried corn were stored for the animals, the springhouse where this morning's milk stood cooling in tall metal cans, and the smokehouse where dark haunches of meat hung from the beams. He made a wide circle around the sty where Ben and Danny were each raising a pig, passed the empty tobacco shed, and headed for the two-story barn. He stopped in the cowshed on the lower floor and decided that he would ask Gideon to show him how to milk one of the black-and-white cows. Then he visited the stables to say some encouraging words to Goldie and to admire Gideon's beautiful horse, Lightning.

Lonely with no one around to talk to, his ankle aching from his rambling inspection of the farm, Isaac found a comfortable spot to rest in the cool shadows of the upper floor of the barn. Leaning against a bale of hay, he watched motes of dust dance in the sunlight. The windows of the house were open, and the haunting sounds of the wailing hymns spilled out into the still morning air, alternating with the old preacher's reedy voice.

Isaac felt drowsy. He was drifting off when he heard a noise and opened his eyes. He was surprised to see Gideon, and Gideon seemed just as surprised to see him. "Sneaking out of the preaching, eh, Isaac?"

"Like you, I guess," Isaac replied.

Gideon laughed a little. "*Ach,* yes, like me. Do your people have something like this? A church or something you go to?" He sat down on a bale of hay and chewed on a stem of grass.

"A *shul,*" Isaac said. "A synagogue. It's a separate building, though, not in somebody's house."

Gideon shoved some hay around with his foot. "Have you been baptized then?"

"I don't know what baptized means."

"It means becoming a member. Joining, like."

"Must be like a *bar mitzvah,*" Isaac

said. "Not yet. In September, when I'm thirteen. You must be able to read the scriptures in Hebrew. I'm still learning." He grimaced, remembering the hours he would have to spend poring over his lessons in *cheder* as soon as he got home. Reb Horowitz, the *melamed,* always rapped his knuckles with a ruler when he made a mistake.

Gideon nodded. "With us it's High German. That's what our Bible is printed in, and it's what Dawdy is preaching in right now—not the Dutch we talk every day. And you want to do this, do you? Be a member? Like being a grown-up?"

"Sure. I never thought about *not* doing it." Isaac looked at Gideon curiously. "Are you . . . what you call it . . . baptized?"

"Not yet. Datt's after me to do it soon. I don't know if I'm going to, though. Everything changes after that. Lots of rules, and if you don't follow them, too bad!" Gideon was silent for a minute, and Isaac wondered what happened to people who didn't follow the rules. "I have an uncle," Gideon went on, "Datt's brother, who left because he didn't want to follow all the rules. Aaron cut his hair a little too short, and then he cut off some of his hat brim. Because of that they put him under the ban and shunned him. Everybody stopped talking to him, even his own family. Datt wouldn't talk to him. Mawmy and Dawdy wouldn't. His own parents! It was like he was dead. I think about that," Gideon said.

Isaac didn't know what to say. He couldn't imagine what that would be like—not having your own family talk to you. *It would be hard,* he thought. *Too hard.* You wouldn't go through that unless it was for something very important. Isaac thought again of cutting off his *payess.* Was cutting off earlocks like cutting a hat brim? More serious? Less serious? Isaac picked up a straw and began chewing it, like Gideon.

"Your people have a lot of rules, too, I've seen that," Gideon said. "Can't eat this, don't eat that. Don't you ever get fed up with the rules and want to leave it all? Or is it different for a Jew?"

"The earlocks," Isaac confessed. He raised the borrowed hat, and the dark strands of hair tumbled down. "They show you're somebody different, an immigrant, not an American. I think about cutting mine off, but my parents wouldn't like it." *But they wouldn't stop talking to me,* he thought. *Would they?*

"I know, I know," Gideon agreed. "You want to look *englische,* and they say no. *Ach,* yes, I know about that. Sometimes," he added slowly, "I think about leaving. Going someplace else to live, to get away from all the rules. I'm waiting for a letter from my uncle. He lives out in Big Valley now, in another county. About a hundred miles from here."

Suddenly the dark form of a broad-chested man in a tailcoat and wide black hat loomed in the wide doorway of the barn, and Gideon got slowly to his feet. The man's face was shadowed, but Isaac recognized the great red beard and the ominous voice as he spoke to Gideon. There was something scary about Ezra, Isaac thought. He was so stern, so severe, not like Tateh—never in the world like Tateh. Isaac saw the defiance in Gideon's eyes. Nevertheless, Gideon dusted off his pants and followed his father's rigid back toward the house.

Isaac wondered what would happen to Gideon. He reminded Isaac of Abie—a rebel. "This isn't the *shtetl*," Abie was always saying to him. "This is America." Gideon's people lived a *shtetl* kind of life even though they'd been here for a long time. Even their grandparents had been born here! Most of them didn't seem to want to change. But Gideon did.

The sun was directly overhead when people began to stream out of the house, and the quiet farm suddenly buzzed with activity. Men handed wooden benches out through the windows; others shoved them together to form tables under the apple trees. Annie and the other girls set the tables with bowls and cups, spoons and knives. Women hurried out of the kitchen with dishes of food and arranged them down the center of the tables.

It had been a long time since breakfast. Isaac edged closer. "We eat last," Ben said, coming up behind Isaac. "Bean soup with ham." He grinned. "But there's always plenty of red beet eggs."

Isaac rolled his eyes. Eat *treyf* or eat eggs—such a choice.

Ben and Isaac perched on the fence rail by the horses, waiting their turn. There were dozens of people ahead of them, but it didn't take long to serve them. Three or four people shared each bowl of soup. Rebecca walked up and down with a kettle and Annie carried a ladle, filling up the bowls as they were emptied. When one group finished eating, the cups and spoons were replaced with a clean set, and another group sat down.

"Won't they run out of food?" Isaac asked.

"Never have."

Finally one of the women yoo-hooed to the youngest boys, and they rushed to the table with Isaac hobbling as fast as he could travel with his aching ankle.

Each table had several large *schnitz*

pies—full-sized moons cut in wedges—and loaves of bread with saucers of chilled butter and pretty china dishes full of bright-colored jams, shimmering jellies, and thick apple butter and glass dishes with cucumber pickles. And a crock of red beets and eggs.

When everyone had finished, the men packed the hymnals into wooden storage trunks and loaded the trunks and the benches onto the wagon that would take them to someone else's farm for the next preaching in two weeks. That chore done, the men were free to discuss the matter that seemed to interest them all: what to do about the peddler's wagon. A dozen of them walked over to the ditch where the wagon still lay. Isaac hobbled along and tried to listen, but he understood almost nothing of the plans that were being made.

It was late afternoon when the last of the procession of buggies disappeared down the long lane in a swirl of dust. Datt and the boys went out to milk before they sat down to their Sunday supper. Mamm's sister and her family and Mawmy and Grossdawdy had stayed, as well as a few neighbors. Gideon and his father didn't look at each other as the chicken and mashed potatoes and gravy were passed. It seemed that Gideon and Ezra were not just silent but were shut up in separate rooms.

CHAPTER 12

The singing's at our house tonight," Annie informed Isaac after supper.

"Singing?" The Sabbath was certainly not a day of rest for the people who had the preaching at their house, Isaac thought. And it wasn't over yet.

"It's a get-together," Annie explained. "I'm not old enough yet to be running around with a fellow, but Mamm says I can help serve the snacks. Come out to the barn with me and we'll watch them. Come on, Isaac," she coaxed, "it'll be fun."

The idea of watching somebody else have a good time didn't interest Isaac much. But Annie wanted him to and so, in the end, Isaac agreed.

Gideon and Levi swept the threshing floor on the upper story of the barn, set up a long table, and arranged benches on two sides. Rebecca had saved some *schnitz* pies from the lunch, and their closest neighbor, Amelia Beiler, brought over the taffy her girls had made.

Isaac watched the arrival of this new procession. There were no sober gray-topped family buggies this evening, but a string of open bachelor buggies racing up the lane. As they pulled into the barnyard, Annie identified the boys who drove and the girls who came with them. "A boy brings his sisters, but then he goes home with the girl he's courting," Annie explained. "When I turn fifteen, or maybe even fourteen, and Datt gives permission, Gideon will take me to the singing, or Levi will, if him and Nancy aren't married yet but I think they will be. Then some other fellow will bring me home after."

Annie found them a place to watch from, behind the bales of straw where Isaac had spent part of the morning talking to Gideon. From there they had a good view of the table, and nobody would pay any attention to them if they hunkered down low and kept quiet.

The boys sat on one side of the table with the girls across from them, and for a while they joked around, teasing each other, it seemed to Isaac, although they were talking Dutch and he didn't catch most of it. "So what's this about singing?" Isaac whispered impatiently.

"See, they've all got hymn books—*Das dinn Bichli,* 'The Thin Book,' it's called. They'll sing songs from those books. You'll see."

Then one of the boys, a skinny fellow with curly hair, made an announcement and they all opened their books and started singing. *At least,* Isaac thought, *it sounds more cheerful than the mournful hymns they chanted during the preaching service.*

Somebody else called out a number and they sang that one, and then another. Late in the evening they stopped singing, much to Isaac's relief. He was tired of it and didn't want to watch anymore.

"Now they eat," Annie whispered. "I've got to go help the girls bring out some snacks. Wait here, I'll get us something." She skittered away and came back with a dish of popcorn and some pieces of taffy for Isaac.

"They'll start to leave soon. Watch and you can see who's courting." She nudged him with her elbow. "See, there's Levi and Nancy Esh. Gideon will drive her sister, Lizzie, home. He's been taking her home from singings for a long time now. I sure wish he'd marry Lizzie," Annie sighed.

Gideon, married? Isaac couldn't imagine it. "Isn't he too young to get married?"

"I mean someday."

Isaac watched, although he didn't much care about who left with whom or who married whom. He kept an eye on Gideon, though, who seemed to be in no particular hurry to get his girl and leave. A fellow Annie said was Crist Miller gave Gideon a hand collecting the "Thin Books" into wooden boxes and putting them on the wagon. Then they stacked the benches onto the wagon, too. After the work was done, the two remained deep in conversation, leaving Lizzie standing by herself. Isaac saw the skinny boy with the curly hair come up to Lizzie and start talking to her. Lizzie kept looking in Gideon's direction, but Gideon went on talking to Crist as though he had forgotten all about her. Then Lizzie seemed to make up her mind about something. A moment later Lizzie Esh left the singing with the curly-haired boy.

"Looks like you were wrong about Lizzie," Isaac said, yawning sleepily. "I guess she doesn't want to marry Gideon. There she goes with somebody else."

"That's Daniel Lapp! Oh, Isaac! Oh, this makes me so angry!" Annie sputtered. "She wants to marry Gideon, I'm sure of it. But he's just so stubborn! Gideon would rather talk to Crist Miller about some foolishness, and now Lizzie's just gotten fed up and left with Daniel."

"But if he's leaving," Isaac suggested, "maybe he doesn't want to marry *her*."

It was the wrong thing to say to Annie,

who burst into tears. Isaac held up a warning hand: Crist had gone, and now Gideon was alone.

"Lizzie?" Gideon said quietly, and then a little louder, "Lizzie! *Lizzie!*" He peered around the barn, whistling a tune, one of the songs they'd been singing. Isaac remembered how Ezra had barked at *him* about whistling on the Sabbath. But Gideon didn't know there was anyone around to hear him. Still whistling, Gideon picked up the kerosene lantern and started to leave.

Suddenly Ezra Stoltzfus appeared in the barn. He was carrying a buggy whip. Annie grabbed Isaac's arm.

Ezra's face was dark as blood, and veins stood out on his neck. He was shouting. Isaac didn't understand the words, but he recognized the fury in Ezra's voice. Annie clutched Isaac's arm tighter, and her nails dug into his skin.

Gideon stood with his arms loose at his sides, his fingers curling and uncurling, and kept his eyes on the dusty floor of the barn. Occasionally he would answer Ezra in a low, hoarse voice. Without warning Ezra raised his arm. The lash of the whip snaked out and curled around Gideon's shoulders with a sickening crack.

Gideon didn't utter a sound. It was as though the whip had not touched him. He stepped forward and wrenched the whip out of his father's hand. Ezra stared at Gideon, his eyes bulging and his mouth working. Then he turned and stalked out. Gideon looked at the buggy whip for a moment before he threw it down and kicked it angrily across the barn floor. He grabbed the lantern and strode out of the barn.

Annie leaped out of their hiding place and ran after him, sobbing, "No, Gideon! Gideon, wait!" Isaac was left alone and trembling.

Gideon set down the lantern and licked his lips. "Now you see, don't you, Annie, why I'm leaving?" he said.

"But why is Datt so mad at you?" Annie asked.

"He caught me skipping out of the

preaching this morning," Gideon replied.

"You weren't there? I thought you were in the other room."

"I was out in the barn. Talking to Isaac about what it's like to be a Jew, and such." Gideon's throat was dry as dust. "There wasn't much he could do to me with Isaac there. He waited until he thought everybody had left tonight to have it out with me."

"But you could have talked to Isaac any time!" Annie cried. "You should have been with us, Gideon. Dawdy was preaching. It must make Datt feel awful bad that you weren't there."

Gideon sighed, feeling ashamed. "Don't you start in on me, too, Annie." He would have given anything if she hadn't been in the barn when Datt came after him. He tried to explain. "Datt says I'm defying him, but I don't see that it's defying him not to want to chain myself to that particular *Ordnung* for the rest of my life. But he won't listen. He says the devil's got me and it's his duty to drive the devil out of me. I've had enough, Annie.

It's not going to change. I got just about everybody down on me now—Dawdy, Datt, Amos, even Levi. You can't imagine how Levi lectures me about my belief, now that he's baptized. You're just about the only friend I have left. You and Crist."

"Crist!" Annie snorted. "Is he the one who got you the *englische* clothes?"

"He knew where I could get them cheap," Gideon replied.

"And is he going with you? Are you planning this together?"

"Crist doesn't have any part in it. Crist likes to do all kinds of wild things, but he doesn't want to leave. He gets along good with his Datt. He'll have that farm some day, and he says he doesn't care about the *Ordnung*. He'll promise whatever the elders want him to and worry about it later."

"Oh, Gideon! I think the devil truly did get into Crist!"

"No more than the devil got into me." Gideon looked away. "You go on in now, Annie. No sense in you getting in trouble, too. I'll be in after a bit."

Gideon watched Annie make her way toward the house, where the soft yellow light in the kitchen had just gone out, signaling that everybody was to be in bed.

"Gideon?" Isaac stepped out of the shadows.

"What are you doing out here? I thought you were upstairs in bed."

"I was in the barn just now," Isaac said. "I saw what happened."

Gideon sighed. "We've all gotten our share of smackings, Isaac," Gideon said, trying to shrug it off. "I'll bet you have, too. Doesn't your Datt get mad at you sometimes, too?"

Isaac shook his head. "Not like that." Gideon tried to ease the boy toward the house, but Isaac would not be moved. "I understand why you want to leave," Isaac said, "but I don't know which is harder, going away or staying here."

"I don't either," Gideon confessed. "But after tonight I don't have a choice. I can't stay. Now the only question is *when* to go."

CHAPTER 13

Isaac lay in bed in the room he was still sharing with the Stoltzfus brothers and listened to the silence. It must have been very late when Gideon crept upstairs. Ben and Danny had fallen asleep, but Isaac guessed that Gideon and Levi were still awake—they turned restlessly, punched their pillows—and he was pretty sure that Annie was lying sleepless in her bed across the hall. When Isaac listened for Ezra's steady snores to come from the spare room, there was only silence.

Isaac remembered nights like this at home when something bad had happened, or was about to happen. The night after the attack on his grandfather in the *shtetl*, all was quiet, but the usual comforting night sounds—Mameh sighing in her sleep, his sisters murmuring as they dreamed, Tateh grunting as he turned over, the sounds that meant everyone was safe—were missing. The family had snatched occasional scraps of troubled sleep throughout the dark night and rose the next morning exhausted, aching in every bone. He recalled other sleepless times like this, before they left the *shtetl* for America and before they moved from New York to Lancaster, when it seemed the long night would never end and then was suddenly over before anyone was ready.

That was how it felt now: everyone was awake, waiting for morning and dreading it.

Isaac wanted to forget the angry scenes he had witnessed, but he couldn't. It was none of his business. He was here entirely by accident. But these people were kind to him. They had salvaged every bit they could of Tateh's merchandise. They had cared for Goldie, and they had nursed him back to health, fed him, and given him clothes and a place to sleep. On Tuesday they would fix Tateh's wagon.

Soon he would go home to his family. Isaac missed them terribly. Imagine leaving them and knowing he might never see them again! That's what his parents had done when they left the *shtetl*. That was what Gideon was planning. If Isaac cut off his *payess,* as Abie Siegel had vowed he would in a few months when he turned thirteen, what would happen? Would that be like leaving his family forever? Would it be worth it? Did being more of an American mean being less of a Jew? All night Isaac wrestled with these questions.

The next thing Isaac knew, the household was up and moving about, and Gideon and Levi had already gone out to the barn. Isaac climbed out of bed and pulled on his pants and hurried out after them. He might not be able to help them solve their problems, but he could at least do his share of chores. Mameh had taught him that much. "Do your part, Isaac," she often said.

"What are you doing out here, Isaac?"

Levi asked when he entered the cow-shed.

"I want to learn to milk. My wrist is fine now," he said, showing how he could move it.

Ezra glanced at him. "Huh," he grunted and jerked his chin toward Gideon.

"Sit down here," Gideon said. He showed Isaac how to balance on the low, three-legged stool and lean a shoulder against the black-and-white cow's warm flank, how to hold a teat in each hand and squeeze and pull them rhythmically. But nothing happened.

"It doesn't work," Isaac complained.

"Keep trying," Gideon advised.

Ezra, Levi, and Gideon moved down the row of cows, wordlessly filling their pails with frothy milk, while Isaac struggled with the same cow, who turned her head to gaze at him. He was rapidly losing patience. He wanted to quit, but stubbornly he kept at it until he finally managed to squirt a fine stream of milk into the pail. Gradually, half an inch of milk gathered in the bottom of the pail, then more. Gideon came to check on him. "That's all she's got," Isaac said. But Gideon sat down and effortlessly stripped one more pint from the silky udder.

"You're catching on," Gideon said encouragingly.

When Isaac came in from the barn an hour later, rubbing his aching fingers, Rebecca Stoltzfus was taking a pan of half-moon *schnitz* pies out of the oven. "These are with butter, especially for you, Isaac." She gave him a hot one for breakfast and showed him where she would put the rest, on the bottom shelf of the pie safe. "So you'll remember which ones are yours."

Breakfast was nearly silent. But, Isaac thought, that's the way it was in this family—no debates at the table, like Tateh thrived on; no neighborhood gossip, which Mameh loved. When they talked at meals in this family, it was only about the work they were planning for that day. Levi and Gideon put the downstairs partitions back in place and brought the furniture in from the shed while Ben and Danny helped Annie fill wooden boxes with tobacco seedlings. Ezra hitched up the three huge draft horses and drove them out to the field. Rebecca and Annie got busy with the wash. It was as though nothing had happened. But underneath the calm surface Isaac felt the tension—Annie's pale face, Rebecca's worried look, Ezra's stiff jaw, Gideon's troubled eyes. Even little Katie, who, like a weather vane, often seemed to be in the same mood as her father, was dark and stormy.

With the currycomb Gideon had given him, Isaac retreated to the quiet of the barn to groom Goldie. He knew the horses by name, had gotten to know their characters as well—Gideon's Lightning was high-spirited but calmed down as soon as Isaac touched him; Robin, who belonged to Levi, was even-tempered; and Midnight, Ezra's buggy horse, had sudden bursts of bad temper that kept Isaac at a distance. *Interesting,* Isaac mused, *how much these horses resembled their owners.* But when he looked at

Goldie, the notion perplexed him. "You're an exception to the rule," Isaac told her. He had begun to feel a loyalty to the old horse; they had shared the same misfortune and now the same recovery, and he had promised her that even when the day came that Tateh could afford another horse to pull his wagon, Isaac would make sure Goldie stayed.

Before noon the family came in for dinner, ate with few words, rested a little, and then went back to work. The day was hot and muggy, and the men's white shirts showed dark patches of sweat. Late in the afternoon it was milking time again. Isaac didn't ask if he could help; he just did. It got a little easier, and he coaxed a little more milk out of the cow, leaving less for Gideon to strip.

They gathered for another almost silent supper, mush with milk and a puddle of melting butter. Even the younger children seemed subdued. It was still daylight when everyone retired, all sleeping in their usual beds now. Once again Isaac was alone in the spare room, thinking of his parents, his sisters, the new baby, his home, and wondering when he would see them. It had been ten days since the wagon was smashed, six since the baby was born. The *bris,* the circumcision, would be on Wednesday, the eighth day. Isaac would miss it. Two Sabbaths and now this. Everything important in his family was going on without him, and even the thought of the bragging he would do to Abie Siegel about his adventures among the *goyim,* the gentiles, wasn't much solace.

On Tuesday as they were finishing breakfast, Annie ran to the window. "Look, Isaac," she said, "here come the neighbors to fix the wagon."

Two sturdy draft horses hauled a hay wagon which was loaded with the battered remains of Tateh's wagon. A group of men carrying tools walked beside it, as though they were accompanying a coffin. The tall, stooped one was John Lapp and the young man was his son, Eli, Annie said. Isaac wondered if this was the same

Lapp family who'd given him the molasses cookies. Next were Menno Fisher and his twin sons, Abe and Abner. Then Daniel Miller, known as Curly Dan, and another Daniel Miller, no relation, known as Salty Dan, because he had once put salt instead of sugar into his coffee at a barn raising, and Salty Dan's nephew Crist Miller.

"I didn't know Crist was coming," Annie said to Gideon. Isaac knew by her frown that she didn't think much of that.

"He's a good worker," Gideon said. "Handy with tools."

Behind them were Joseph Esh, Nancy's and Lizzie's father, and their neighbor Reuben Beiler and his father, Zeke. Last to arrive was Amos, racing up the lane in a swirl of dust.

"Where's Barbara?" Annie wondered aloud, sounding disappointed. "She told Mamm she'd help out with the lunch."

But Amos explained that Davy was colicky, and Barbara thought it better to keep him at home.

Before the men started on the wagon, Rebecca Stoltzfus fed them a snack of coffee soup—coffee and cream poured over bread, sprinkled with sugar. "Can't ask a man to work on an empty stomach," she said.

Meanwhile Amos helped Gideon and Levi haul lumber out of the shed and set up wooden sawhorses in the side yard. When they had finished eating, the men heaved the broken wagon onto the sawhorses. The older men walked around the wagon and studied it, discussing it in low murmurs. Isaac knew that Gideon had studied it the day they went out to the ditch with the wheelbarrow, but Gideon wasn't given a chance to say anything now—Ezra did the talking and divided up the jobs.

The two wheels that had spun off were both damaged, as were the two still on the wagon. Ezra decided, and the others agreed, that the wheelwright was the likely one to fix them all. The four wheels were loaded onto Ezra's spring wagon, and Gideon hitched up one of the draft horses and set off for the wheelwright's shop in Intercourse. Isaac thought he must be glad to get away from his Datt's fierce eyes.

Reuben Beiler removed the remains of the wooden boxes where Tateh had kept his merchandise and set to work repairing the hardware and replacing the damaged parts.

The Fisher twins examined the axletree and began to make a new one, shaping a rough timber to the correct size with their adzes and then smoothing it with their planes. The shafts to which Goldie had been harnessed were also a total loss, and they were replaced with two strong, new poles.

Salty Dan and Crist sawed boards and nailed them in place along the sides of the wagon bed.

Isaac watched anxiously, wanting to help. But there was nothing he could do but fetch water from the pump when the men got thirsty.

At noon they stopped for dinner. A makeshift table was set up under a shade tree, and Rebecca and Annie served fried ham, baked beans, coleslaw, cucumber pickles, bread and butter, and grape jelly. And pickled red beets and eggs.

The men ate first, not wasting any time in conversation except to joke with Salty Dan when the coffeepot was passed around. After the men had gone back to work, Isaac and Ben and Danny sat down at the table with Annie and her mother. Rebecca reminded Isaac of his plate of special *schnitz* pies. He pushed the plate toward Annie. "Have one."

She shook her head. "They're yours," she said. Her sad smile told him what he had not been able to ask: nothing had been resolved with Gideon.

Reuben Beiler finished putting new hinges and latches on the boxes he had rebuilt, and John Lapp and Menno Fisher screwed them down to the wagon bed. Zeke Beiler made a new seat, even though the old one hadn't been damaged. Joseph Esh mended the harness and reins.

Late in the afternoon Gideon returned with the wheels, and the men lifted them into place. Gideon seemed agitated; Isaac noticed that when he tried to tighten the bolts on the wheels, he was all thumbs. Ezra yelled at him, and Amos finished the tightening. If Gideon minded being yelled at, he didn't let on.

When the wagon stood on its own again, it looked almost the same as it had when Tateh brought it home, except for the raw new lumber. The men stood around it, quietly admiring their work. Isaac joined them, feeling he needed to say something, to thank them or to find out what the charge would be, but he didn't know how to begin. The men put away their tools and got ready to leave.

Then Grossdawdy, who had spent the day watching but leaving the actual work to the younger men, spoke up. "Look better if it was painted," he said.

Ezra disappeared into the toolshed and came back with a bucket of black paint. "Black is all we've got," he said to Isaac. "What do you think?"

"Black is good," Isaac said.

Ezra had brought two paintbrushes, the bristles worn but still usable. He gave one to Isaac, one to Ben. "Start now, and you'll be done by dark," Ezra said, "if you don't fool around."

Then Rebecca rushed out from the kitchen, inviting everyone to stay for a snack. "Just a piece before you go," she urged. "Can't send you home hungry."

Without any protest the men went back to the makeshift table under the shade tree for coffee and shoofly pie. But Isaac was eager to paint. He started with the new seat.

Ben began at the opposite end of the wagon. "We'll meet in the middle," he said and Isaac agreed, until they realized there was only one bucket of paint. Then they worked side by side.

"Here's a question for you, Isaac," Ben said, slapping paint on the sideboards. "If a rooster lays an egg on top of the barn, which side will it fall down?"

Isaac thought about that. "I give up," he said.

"A rooster doesn't lay eggs!" Ben shouted and hooted with laughter.

"That's stupid," Isaac said.

"No, it's not—it's funny. Here's

another one: Which side of the chicken has the most feathers?"

"I don't know. Which?"

"The outside!"

Isaac dripped some black paint on his pants—the ones he had worn for whitewashing the outhouse. Then he forgot that he had paint on his hand and smeared some on his face.

"Looks like a mustache," said Ben.

"You want one too?" Isaac asked, brandishing his brush.

Ben ducked away. "We're not allowed to have mustaches."

"Why not? The men all have beards."

"Beards are for married men. But no mustaches, no matter."

"That doesn't make sense."

Ben shrugged. "Doesn't have to." Then he grinned. "Mustaches are like buttons. Just another rule—like pig fat, I guess. Now *that* doesn't make sense."

"Sure it does. It makes more sense not to eat lard than it does not to wear buttons or mustaches."

"To you it does. Not to me."

"Do you get tired of all your rules?" Isaac asked.

"Don't think about it much. What about you?"

"I guess sometimes I get tired of them." *But not enough to run away,* he added silently.

It was almost dark when they ran out of paint, and the wagon was finished. It looked magnificent, Isaac decided—if not exactly magnificent, then much, *much* better than it had before the accident. Rebecca clucked her tongue when she saw the boys and got coal oil to clean off the paint splatters.

Ezra inspected their work. "It's ready to go, Isaac," he said, "whenever your Datt comes for it. I believe the horse is mended, too, is she not, Gideon?"

As far as Isaac knew, it was the first time Ezra had spoken calmly to Gideon since Sunday.

Gideon nodded. "Instead of waiting for his Datt to come for him," he said, "I could drive him in the wagon into Lancaster City later this week. If you can spare me," he added, staring at his shoes.

"It's all the same to me," Ezra grunted, turning his back.

"But how would you get home again, Gideon?" Rebecca asked.

"On the trolley." He avoided his mother's eyes, too.

"Make it Thursday then," Ezra said.

Day after tomorrow! One more day, Isaac thought with relief, *and I'll be going home!* But when Isaac glanced at Annie and saw the panic all over her face, he knew that much more was bothering her than his going. Suddenly Isaac caught on: Gideon was planning to use the trip to Lancaster as his excuse to leave.

"I wonder if that's a good idea, taking the wagon," Annie was saying. Gideon glared at her, but she paid no attention. "Suppose Peddler Jakob has decided to come out here and pick up Isaac and Goldie and the wagon, and he's already on his way, and he gets here and finds out you've left and you're on your way to Lancaster. Maybe it would be better to wait."

But it was Ezra who agreed that it would be a good thing for Gideon to drive into Lancaster City with the wagon. "You can do some errands for me while you're there," he said. "I need some new tools. I saw how bad my plane acted when we worked on the wagon."

"I could go, too," Annie blurted out. "If there's not too much work to do, if you could spare me," she hurried on, looking pleadingly at her mother. "I could do errands for you, too. We could go to the market and bring back whatever you need."

But Datt shook his head. "No. No need for you to be riding on any trolley."

Annie silently bowed her head. *Poor Annie,* Isaac thought. *I wish I could think of a way to help her.*

"One more riddle, Isaac," Ben coaxed. "What will come but never arrive?"

"I give up."

"Tomorrow!"

CHAPTER 14

Annie and Mamm, with help from Ben and Danny, packed the salvaged goods into the new boxes on the wagon. Isaac decided where everything was to go. The clothes Isaac had worn at the time of the wreck had been carefully mended and patched, and they were now wrapped in the blanket and oilcloth that had made up his bedroll. Mamm had baked another panful of special *schnitz* pies, and she was sending a loaf of bread and a dozen eggs and some of her finest preserves as a gift to Isaac's mother in honor of the new baby. It was Ben's idea to include a crock of red beet eggs, "to show your Mamm what you've been eating all along." Isaac tried to protest, but he was too polite to turn down the gift outright, and so the eggs were packed, too.

Annie paced restlessly, trying to convince herself that she was wrong, that Gideon really was going to take Isaac and the wagon to Lancaster City, buy Datt's tools, and come back on the trolley, just as he said. Maybe she was upset for nothing, although it *did* seem he always made sure she couldn't catch him alone. And how Annie wished she'd had a chance to talk to Barbara about all of this!

Ever since she and Isaac had witnessed the awful scene in the barn, Annie had not known what to say to Isaac. She hated having him see Datt lose his temper like that. But when she was in the chicken coop after supper, gathering eggs into her apron, Isaac found her there. "Maybe you could come visit me sometime," he said. "Mameh would make you some wonderful food."

"Maybe." Annie shooed one of the hens off her nest and collected two warm, brown eggs.

"It was nice to be here," Isaac said. "You were all good to me."

"No trouble. We didn't do anything extra." She took the eggs and ran into the house, leaving Isaac alone with the chickens.

That night Annie lay awake, her thoughts pursuing one another in circles, like angry cats. Gideon was four years older, but in many ways he was like a twin brother. When Gideon left, she would lose part of herself. Yet when she remembered the look of fury on Datt's face as he raised the buggy whip and the sickening crack as the whip struck Gideon, Annie knew that she could not ask her brother to abide that treatment much longer.

Still, it wasn't *much* longer—it was just a *little* longer! In a few more years Gideon would be married and farming on his own nearby, like Amos was now and Levi would be as soon as he married Nancy. Even if Datt didn't help Gideon buy a place right away, Gideon could farm for somebody else as a tenant for a while. Then he and Datt wouldn't be working together day after day and fighting all the time.

If he'd just get baptized like Levi did! Before Levi was baptized, he'd gotten his share of smackings, too. Joining the church usually made boys settle down and quit running wild, the way some did— like Crist.

Maybe it was Crist who put Gideon up to this; Annie had seen them with their heads together when they were working on the wagon. Crist had gotten a lot of smackings from his Datt, and Annie didn't doubt for a minute that he deserved them. Most boys needed a smacking at some time or other to straighten them out— even Amos had—although she wasn't sure the punishment had done Crist much good; he was seventeen and still being wild.

And how could Gideon just go off and leave Mamm and all of them, the farm, everything? Annie would never think of leaving. How *could* he? It made her awful mad at him. But she knew that nothing she said would change his mind. He hadn't promised to tell her when he was going. "You'll know"—that was all he'd said.

There was one way to tell: check the hidey-hole and see if the *englische* clothes were still there.

Annie made sure that Katie was sleeping deeply and slipped quietly out of the room. She stole softly down the hall to the spare room where Isaac was spending his last night in this house. Annie stopped and listened to Isaac's breathing. It was slow and even. Step by careful step she moved closer, sank to her hands and knees, and crawled the last few feet to the bed. She stretched flat on her stomach and wriggled, one muscle at a time, to get far enough under the bed so that she could reach the nail. Almost, almost . . .

A face peered at her, upside down. "Annie?" Isaac whispered. "Is that you? What are you doing?"

"Hush," she whispered back. "Yes, it's me. I'm looking for something."

She found the nail and lifted out the loose boards and quietly set them aside. Then she reached down into the space. It was empty. The clothes were gone.

Isaac knelt on the floor beside her. "What is it, Annie?"

Annie pounded her fist softly on the floor. "Gideon kept his *englische* clothes hidden in here, and now they're gone. When he takes you into Lancaster City, he means to keep on going and not come back here at all. This proves it."

"Maybe he just moved them to a safer place," Isaac suggested. "Maybe he knew you found them, and he hid them someplace else."

She shook her head. "I'll show you where I think they are. Then you'll believe me. Come on, Isaac."

She led the way downstairs, showing him how to step on the sides of the stairs to keep them from squeaking. Noiselessly she crossed the kitchen and held open the screen door for Isaac. Safely outside, she ran down the path—Isaac limping a little but keeping up—through Mamm's garden and around the barnyard to the shed where Datt stored his farming tools and where the peddler's wagon stood gleaming in its new coat of paint. "You look in the boxes on that side," Annie instructed Isaac, "and I'll look in these."

It didn't take her long to find what she feared, folded beneath one of the lengths of cloth that Mamm had washed and ironed. She pulled them out and held them up for Isaac to see—trousers, jacket, shirt, suspenders, necktie, cap. In the jacket pocket was the mouth organ, and *Treasure Island* had been wrapped in the middle of the bundle. "See? I told you! I've got to find some way to stop him. It's not right for him to go! Things will get better if he stays, I know they will!"

"But what can you do, Annie?" Isaac asked. "Tell your Datt? He'd stop him, all right."

"I don't know." She wiped her eyes on the sleeve of her nightdress. "What do you think I should do, Isaac?" she asked.

Isaac didn't answer right away. He

seemed to be thinking it over. Finally he said, "I know you're worried about Gideon leaving, but I don't think you can do anything about it. Seems like he's made up his mind he's going, and nothing you say or do is going to stop him. If you tell your Datt, that would cause more trouble. Your Datt would get out the buggy whip again, and Gideon would just wait for another chance to run away. It looks like him and your Datt don't get along so good. Maybe it would be better for Gideon, and for your Datt too, if he went away for a while. I guess if it was my brother, or my sister, somebody old enough to know what he wants to do, I guess I'd just say good-bye."

"It's true, they don't get along," Annie admitted. Then she tried to explain to Isaac why it mattered so much. "But if Gideon goes, he'll be lost to us forever. Not just for now, but for all eternity, even after we're all dead. I won't be able to speak to him, ever again." She hurried on, "The elders will put him under the ban, like they did my uncle, Aaron. Every one of us will have to shun my brother. We will be forbidden to speak to him or eat with him or have anything at all to do with him. It will be just like he died, only worse, because then there is no hope of reunion with him after death."

"What if you break the rule and talk to him?" Isaac asked.

"Then I would be shunned, too."

"But what if Gideon decides someday he wants to come back?" Isaac pressed.

"He would have to repent, kneel down in front of the whole church and ask for forgiveness."

"Would they forgive him then?"

"I think so," she said with a sigh. "It's *asking* that's the hard part. Datt's brother Aaron wouldn't ask."

Gideon thought he'd feel calmer. He hadn't really considered what it would be like when the time actually came to leave. And now that the time was here, he was in turmoil. He could hardly eat his supper Wednesday night, and that made him mad at himself because he knew it was the last of Mamm's meals he'd have for a good long time, maybe forever.

It had been a hot, miserable day in the tobacco field. There had been no planting the day before, what with working on the peddler's wagon all day. But the wagon had brought Gideon a remarkable stroke of luck. If Datt had not sent him into Intercourse to the wheelwright's shop, Gideon would not have stopped by Huffnagle's store while he was waiting for the wheels to be fixed.

"Just came in yesterday," Elmer Huffnagle had said, passing the envelope to Gideon.

Gideon had been so nervous and excited, he had torn the letter trying to get it out of the envelope. It was written on lined paper, and it was very short.

"Come on out when you're ready," Aaron had written. "You are more than welcome here. The train stops morning and evening in Lewistown. Belleville is a good piece out from there. Let us know when you're coming and we'll meet you at the depot."

Gideon had sprung onto the buggy seat. "Yo-ho-ho, and a bottle of rum!" he sang out as he drove back to the wheelwright's shop. He was as good as on his way to Big Valley.

Later, back at the farm, Crist had helped Gideon unload the wheels from the wagon. Under his breath Gideon said, "I got the letter from my uncle. Just picked it up at Huffnagle's. My uncle says to come whenever I'm ready. Just to let him know and he'll meet me at the train station."

"When do you plan to leave?" Crist murmured.

"I don't know. I haven't decided."

"And what are you going to tell your folks?"

"I don't know," Gideon repeated.

"Your Datt's sure going to be mad. Like a whole nest of hornets!" Crist warned.

Datt was already bellowing, "Come on, Gideon, get those wheels over here!"

"Same as always," Gideon whispered

to Crist, but his heart was light and he was almost dizzy with excitement.

The lightheartedness and dizziness had lasted through the rest of the day, while they worked on the wagon. And Gideon could hardly believe his second stroke of good luck in one day, when Datt agreed to let him drive Isaac and the wagon to Lancaster. But his joy began to sour when he told Mamm an untruth, letting her think he'd be coming back on the trolley.

And then Annie! Imagine her trying to talk Mamm into letting her go along with him. Annie knew exactly what he was planning. Of course Datt could be counted on to say no. Once a year after the tobacco was sold, the whole family usually traveled to Lancaster for a day of shopping and stopped off to spend the night with relatives on the way home. But Datt generally did not allow his family to travel on the trolley, arguing that to do so was being yoked with the unbeliever, the company that ran the trolleys. Gideon was somewhat surprised that Datt had agreed to let him go this time. There was still the possibility that Datt might change his mind, though even he would not want to disappoint Isaac.

But now the time of his departure was coming, and Gideon was not sure exactly what to do. He still didn't know how much a train ticket would cost to—he got out the letter and checked the name of the town—to Lewistown. He had foolishly spent too much money on his *englische* clothes. If he had put aside the money Barbara had given him for building the fence, he probably would have had enough to buy the ticket.

At last a solution came to him: if he had to, he would sell the book and the mouth organ, his two worldly treasures. They should fetch at least a little, and if he was lucky, enough for a ticket.

Gideon lay in bed, listening to the quiet sounds of the farm. *My last night in this bed,* he thought. *My last night in this room, on this farm.*

This day had been no worse, and no better, than any of the days before it. Datt had little to say, except to tell them that they would not come in for dinner as they usually did. Annie was to bring their dinner out to the field. When Levi had attempted to joke while they rested in the shade of an ancient chestnut tree, Datt had glowered at him and told him not to talk such foolishness. He had rebuked Levi instead of Gideon! And then Datt cut short their rest, so that by the time he finally decided to call it a day, even Gideon was exhausted.

But still Gideon couldn't sleep. He had much too much to think about.

Sometime during the night, Gideon heard a noise, a rattle on the windowpane. He lay still, breathing lightly, listening. Then he heard the noise again, followed by a low whistle. It was Crist's signal. Gideon pulled on his pants and hurried downstairs.

"I came to say good-bye," Crist said.

"Well," Gideon said, caught off guard by the surge of emotion he felt.

"You'll come back some day," Crist ventured. It was partly a question, partly a statement.

"Maybe. I don't know. I have to see how it goes."

Crist cleared his throat. "All right, then." He turned to go.

"Where's your rig?" Gideon asked.

"At the end of the lane. I didn't want to make a racket."

"I'll walk down with you then."

There had been no rain for days and the lane was carpeted with powdery dust.

"I have a favor to ask," Gideon said when they reached Crist's rig.

"Sure."

"Take care of Annie, will you? Just keep an eye on her? And Mamm, too. They'll put me under the *Meidung* when they find out where I went, and she won't be allowed to write to me. But you could write. Send it in care of Aaron Stoltzfus in Belleville."

"But I'll be observing the *Meidung* too, Gideon. Did you forget that?"

Gideon hadn't thought about that. Of course he knew that Crist was subject to the same *Ordnung* as everybody else in their district. But somehow he hadn't thought his old friend who'd raised so much Cain would obey the rule and shun him too. "You won't write, then?"

Crist shook his head. "Can't. I'm to be baptized soon, myself. But I will look after your sister. I promise you that." Crist shook his hand and then turned away abruptly, climbed into his buggy, and sped away.

So, Gideon thought sadly, watching the cloud of dust, *it has already begun. This is how it's going to be.*

The morning of what Annie believed would be the worst day of her life started out like every other morning, as though it was going to be another ordinary day of June sunshine. Datt and Levi and Gideon went out to milk, and Isaac trailed along. He had gotten better at milking, but it took him as long to do one cow as it took the others to do four. Then Gideon had to strip out the last of the milk anyway.

Mamm had cooked a special breakfast for Isaac, since it was to be his last one with the family—sticky buns studded with English walnuts from the trees in the yard. When Gideon and the others came in from milking, Annie was so nervous and upset that she barely managed to get the food to the table without dropping it. She felt as though she was about to crumble to tiny pieces. Even Datt noticed. "What ails you, girl?" he asked.

"Nothing." She kept her eyes on her plate, not daring to look across the table at Gideon. But when she did manage to glance his way, she saw that he, too, seemed tense. In fact, he spilled his coffee, and there was a flurry of activity as Mamm rushed to find a rag to mop it up.

"Dopplig," Datt grumbled. "Mind you pay attention to the road or you won't have any better luck finding the city than you do your own mouth."

Finally everybody gathered around to say good-bye to Isaac. Datt didn't have much to say—just wished him a safe journey with a curt nod of his head. Levi shook his hand, and so did Ben and Danny, trying to act grown-up. Katie said, "Bye," and hid behind Mamm. Mamm hugged Isaac and told him to give her best regards to his father and mother and the new baby.

When it was Annie's turn to tell Isaac good-bye, all the tears she'd been storing up over Gideon broke loose, and she covered her face with her apron and ran into the house and fell sobbing onto her bed. Now she was furious with herself because she had ruined her chance to say good-bye to Gideon.

"Annie." Gideon was standing uneasily in the doorway.

She sat up and blew her nose. "You're leaving," she said flatly. "You're not coming back on the trolley like you said."

"No, I'm not coming back. I got a letter from Aaron," he said. "It's better if I go out to Big Valley. You saw how it is with me and Datt."

Annie tried another approach. "What about Lizzie?" she asked shakily. "Have you told her you're leaving?"

Gideon shook his head. "I haven't seen

Lizzie since the singing. Crist said she went home with Daniel Lapp."

"But she doesn't care for him! She cares for *you*, Gideon!"

"She'll forget me. She must. You can tell her good-bye for me, Annie. Make her understand why I'm leaving."

"But *I* don't understand! It's only for a little longer! Oh, Gideon, I can't bear for you to leave us forever!"

"Maybe it's not forever. Someday, when I can buy my own place and don't have to work with Datt, maybe then I can come home again."

"Promise me." She wanted to run to him and cling to him until he said the words, but she forced herself to remain still. "Promise me you'll come back."

"I don't make promises I'm not sure I can keep. Annie, believe me, this is hard for me, too. It's not that I don't care about all of you—even Datt. I wish we could get along, him and me! I'm not going just for the adventure—I'm going because I have to. If I could, I'd take you with me in a minute, but that wouldn't be right. You belong here. You'll grow up to be an obedient member of the church, the way you should——" Gideon's voice cracked. "But somehow that's not in me. I wish it was."

He's hurting inside as much as I am, Annie thought, and, seeing that his eyes were wet, glistening with tears, she reached out to him. But Gideon was already moving away from her, wiping his eyes with his fingers.

"Good-bye, Annie," he said, his voice trembling.

"Gideon! Gideon!"

He turned and left, his footsteps on the stairs steady and firm. He didn't look back.

Annie watched from the upstairs window as the peddler's wagon, looking almost new, rolled out of the barnyard, drawn by Goldie. Even the old horse held her head up and looked proud to be pulling such a good-looking rig. Isaac perched on the new driver's seat beside Gideon. When they reached the gate, Isaac jumped down and ran to open it, and Gideon drove through. Isaac shut the gate and latched it, waved to Mamm and the younger boys and, Annie thought, to her in the upstairs window, and ran to catch up.

Annie watched until the wagon was out of sight. Then she wiped her face, straightened her cap, and hoping that no one would notice her breaking heart, prepared to face a family that would no longer include Gideon.

CHAPTER 15

"Well, we're on our way now for sure," Gideon said and smiled at Isaac as he flicked the reins across Goldie's rump. "Are you glad to be going home?"

"Sure. But I don't know the way from here. Do you?"

"*Ach,* yes," Gideon said. "Don't worry. I know these roads like the back of my hand."

Of course Isaac was glad. He was anxious to see Mameh and Tateh and his sisters and his new baby brother. He was also looking forward to showing off the fixed-up wagon with its glistening new coat of paint. Even Goldie looked better than she had; two weeks of rest and extra oats and daily grooming had done her good. Isaac could hardly wait for a taste of Mameh's cooking; he hoped that, after she thanked Gideon profusely for the crock of red beet eggs, she would somehow get rid of them, even though he knew Mameh was too thrifty ever to throw away food.

And he'd been rehearsing in his mind the stories he would tell Abie Siegel about his adventures.

There were some things about the past two weeks that Isaac would just as soon forget—mainly Ezra Stoltzfus's bad temper and the trouble it caused. It had threatened to erupt again as Gideon and Isaac were preparing to leave. Ezra's fierce face seemed to glower more darkly than ever as he issued a long list of instructions and warnings to Gideon, who was impatient to get going. Rebecca must have guessed by now that the trouble brewing between Ezra and Gideon had come to a head, but she had to console the tearful Katie, whose kitten was missing. Levi looked solemn. Ben and Danny clowned around for the benefit of Isaac and Gideon, pestering to be taken along, too. Annie had begun to cry and ran to her room. Gideon's decision to use this trip to Lancaster as his chance to leave was clear as rain to Isaac, even though Gideon hadn't said anything directly to him about his intention. Did anyone but Annie guess that Gideon was not coming back?

The scene outside the farmhouse reminded Isaac of the day his family left the *shtetl*. Isaac himself, then a child of nine, had been thrilled about the great adventure ahead—the boat trip, the Golden Country where dreams came true, the enormous city that Tateh had promised him was a thousand times bigger, a thousand times richer, with a thousand times more of everything than their own nearby town of Ukmergé. Mingled with Isaac's excitement had been the sadness of leaving behind dear ones whose grief was almost too much to bear.

Isaac thought that, for Gideon, leaving the farm must be a lot like crossing a vast ocean to a foreign land where his language was not spoken and his ways not understood. Gideon's people who were left behind would mourn—Annie said it was not just that her brother was leaving for a different place but that he would be cut off from them "for all eternity," something Isaac did not quite understand.

Isaac was appalled; it seemed to him unjust and cruel to punish a person so. He had thought so when Gideon, and then Annie, told him what had happened to their uncle. He tried to imagine what it would be like if suddenly everybody in his family turned away from him as if he had ceased to exist. The idea simply made him shudder.

As they rumbled along at Goldie's slow, stately pace, Gideon pointed out landmarks and told Isaac whose farm they were passing. These were neighbors Gideon knew well, many of them related to him in some way. "Now that's Amos's place," he said, pointing out a small farmhouse skirted by a neat white fence. "He's renting from Reuben Beiler—you met Reuben, little short fellow who worked on the wagon—but he'll get his own place soon. Datt will help him, and Barbara's people will pitch in, too."

Soon after they passed Amos's place, they turned off the rutted and dusty Weavertown Road and headed west on the black paved surface of Lincoln Highway toward Lancaster City. "We're out of our district now," Gideon said. "This is a different church district. I don't know folks so well here." He sighed deeply and fell silent.

There was a fair amount of traffic, most of it horse and buggy, but once in a while an automobile passed them. "Wouldn't I like to ride in one of those!" Gideon exclaimed, watching a Ford whiz by. "But I doubt I ever will." He kept a firm hold on the reins in case the machine spooked Goldie. But the old mare seemed not to notice or to mind.

The automobile put an idea into Isaac's head. "It would be just the thing for peddling," he said. "Tateh could put wooden boxes on top for the merchandise. Can't you see me now?" He pretended to steer an automobile. "With a sign on the side that says 'Jakob Litsky and Son, Dry Goods,' painted in red and gold. Don't you think that would look fine?"

Gideon nodded, but his thoughts seemed to be somewhere else.

"And then," Isaac continued, enjoying the chance to talk about his dream, "when my father is old, I'll take over the business myself. And it will say 'Isaac Litsky, Dry Goods.' " He paused, remembering Mameh's thoughts on the matter: *One peddler in the family is enough. For you, Isaac, something else. A better life.* "My mother doesn't want me to, though," Isaac admitted. "She has other plans for me."

"I wouldn't like it much, traveling like that, winter, summer, rain, shine, sleeping in a different place every night," Gideon said. "A person needs a home, a place to be, and not to be traipsing around all the time. A farm, a family, animals, crops to tend—that's a good life."

"But I thought you're leaving that life," Isaac blurted out.

"Annie told you that?"

Isaac nodded.

"*Ach,* well, I think she's wrong. I'm leaving *home,* that's for sure, but not the farm life, not the Amish life. I'm going to my uncle up in Big Valley, in Mifflin County. I got a letter day before yesterday. Aaron, the one they put under the ban. Now they'll shun me, too. That's what's hard."

Isaac nodded sympathetically, and his hands flew up to stroke his *payess.* Every time he thought about Gideon's struggles within himself, Isaac inevitably reflected on his own dilemmas: whether to cut off his *payess;* whether to eat *treyf;* whether to skip *cheder;* whether to become an English-speaking American instead of a Yiddish-speaking foreigner. He thought of the last thing Tateh had said to him: "Remember who you are, Isaac." That was the important thing: *Remember who you are.*

"What are you going to do now?" Isaac asked.

"First, make sure you and Goldie and the wagon get home safe. Next, buy

Datt's tools. Then figure out where to get ahold of some money for train fare."

They plodded steadily toward the city. A hot June sun blazed down on them, and dust streaked their sweaty skin. Gideon wiped his face on his shirtsleeve. Isaac opened a jar of water, drank from it, and passed it to Gideon.

Well before noon they pulled off the pike and stopped under a shade tree to eat the lunch Rebecca had packed for them—Lebanon bologna sandwiches for Gideon, apple butter on bread for Isaac, *schnitz* pies made with butter instead of lard, another jar of water.

Gideon stretched out on the ground and closed his eyes. In a moment he was fast asleep. All morning Isaac had been trying to stay calm, but now they were nearing the city and he was restless and impatient. He felt as though he had been away for a long, long time, although actually only two Sabbaths had passed, less than three weeks. There would be so much to tell his family, so many questions to answer. And Gideon was asleep!

After what seemed like a long time,

Gideon opened his eyes and squinted at the sky. "Time to move on." They let Goldie drink from a trough by the road and drove on.

Although Isaac knew he must have been on this road before, traveling in the opposite direction, he didn't seem to recognize anything. Apparently Gideon was as unfamiliar as Isaac was with the city streets. "Where do we go now?" Gideon asked.

Isaac shook his head. He had no idea which way to turn. But Goldie, who had traveled along these streets every Friday for the past few months, knew exactly where she was going. "This is our street!" Isaac exclaimed as she turned the corner.

"Goldie might be awful slow and maybe not the prettiest horse I ever saw, but she sure knows her way back home," Gideon remarked.

"She is a very smart horse," Isaac announced, realizing this for perhaps the first time. "And she's not that bad looking either."

Tirzah and Leah were playing on the

sidewalk in front of the narrow brick house on Rockland Street. They looked up in surprise as Goldie halted of her own accord, and then the sisters stared in astonishment as Isaac jumped down from the wagon seat. Isaac savored the moment, grinning broadly.

"Isaac!" they squealed and scrambled to greet him, both talking at once in a mixture of Yiddish and English: "Where did you get the new wagon?" "Does Tateh know you are coming?" "Did you know we have a new brother?" "Mameh was ill for a while, but now she is better!" "I will go get her!" "No, I will!" "I will get Tateh, then!"

Still grinning, Isaac turned to Gideon who was climbing slowly down from the wagon seat. "My sisters," he explained.

The girls raced for the front door. But the door had already opened and Tateh peered out, at first curious and then elated. "Isaac!" he exclaimed and opened his arms. Isaac let himself be swept into his father's embrace.

"Essie! Sarah!" Tateh shouted. "Isaac is home! And wait till you see what he has brought with him!" He spun around. "And Isaac! Wait till you see what we have for you here!"

Mameh appeared at the door, leaning on Sarah's arm. *She looks so pale,* Isaac thought, alarmed at his mother's appearance. But then she smiled her familiar smile. Isaac ran to kiss her on the cheek to let her see that he was fine after all, with only a few scrapes and bumps that were now almost entirely mended and a slight limp that he tried not to show.

Meanwhile Tateh was hugging Gideon again and thumping him on the back, fairly dancing in the street. "My wagon!" he sang. "Look, Essie, look at the wagon! It is a miracle, truly a miracle!" He kissed the startled Gideon on both cheeks.

Isaac was a little embarrassed for Gideon to see the exuberant Tateh carrying on like this, so different from dour Ezra Stoltzfus. From where he stood with Mameh's arm looped through his, Isaac could see that Gideon was blushing. "Come, Mameh," Isaac said, "you must meet Gideon."

Gideon blushed again when Sarah was introduced, and he stared down at the toes of his shoes as though his footwear was of great interest.

"And you, Isaac, must meet your new brother. His name is Joshua."

A small bundle with a crown of silky black hair lay in a cradle next to Mameh's bed, eyes closed, rosy mouth puckered. A pair of tiny fists waved in the air.

"Hello, Joshua," Isaac said softly. "Welcome to the family. I think you are going to like it here." He reached down and touched one of the flailing fists, which closed around his finger.

"*Whshht,* Isaac!" Sarah hissed. "You have not even washed your hands!"

"Sorry," Isaac mumbled, pulling his finger away. Dark eyes opened and seemed to peer worriedly at Isaac. The rosebud mouth gaped and let out a howl. Sarah picked up the noisy bundle and rocked him on her shoulder. He immediately quieted. Isaac tiptoed outside.

Now everyone had to walk around the wagon, admiring it from every angle. Tateh examined Goldie's foreleg, and

Gideon explained that it had healed for the most part but was troubling her after her long haul in from the countryside. Next each wooden box had to be opened, the fine carpentry examined, the contents of the boxes marveled over. They unpacked the bread and the eggs and the preserves that Rebecca had sent as a gift. Every other minute, it seemed, Tateh burst out with fresh torrents of praise and thanks and more thumps on Gideon's back.

Mameh was the first to retire to the house, and Sarah was immediately sent out again to invite Gideon to come inside—no, to *insist* that he must come in for a visit and refreshment. The younger girls, Leah and Tirzah, stared at their visitor with frank curiosity, just the way Ben and Danny had stared at Isaac in the beginning. When Tateh announced that he would take Goldie and the wagon around to the shed, Isaac interrupted. "No, I will take them, Tateh," he said. "I have learned to unhitch her. You will see."

"Then permit me to accompany you," Tateh said, grinning broadly and stroking his beard. "I wish to observe this, if you do not mind."

Ah, it's so good to hear Yiddish again, Isaac thought. He had missed it. He had gotten a little better at understanding Dutch, although the Stoltzfuses usually spoke English when he was around. Still, there was nothing so welcome to his ears as the sound of Tateh's Yiddish.

"And you are sure you are absolutely well again?" Tateh asked him over and over. "We were so worried! Yet there was nothing I could do. The new baby, your mother . . . We were both frantic, I can promise you that! I had hoped to come this week for you, your mother insisted that it was time, she was fine and able to do without me. But I was worried about her—because of the last time, on the boat—you understand. And I was worried about you, too! Still, you are back safely, and now everything is fine again!"

Yes, Isaac thought, *in our family, everything is fine.* It was Gideon's people that troubled him.

CHAPTER 16

As soon as Isaac and Gideon were out of sight, Annie came back down from her bedroom and found the kitchen table heaped with rosy strawberries. Mamm was preparing to put up jam.

Mamm had looked her over curiously. "A nice boy, that Isaac," she said. "No doubt you're sad to see him go. We'll all miss him."

"Yes," Annie said, relieved by Mamm's interpretation. She sat down at the table and began hulling berries. Mamm stood at the stove, stirring and skimming the boiling fruit. Clouds of steam pinked her cheeks. They washed the jars saved from the previous year, scalded them, ladled the hot, thick jam into them, sealed them with melted paraffin. As she worked Annie was thinking, *Barbara. I must talk to Barbara.*

"Later," she said to Mamm, "when we're done and I've taken care of the seedlings, I could take some jam to Barbara and Amos."

"That's a good idea, Annie," Mamm said. "It will help you get your mind off Isaac. Ben and Danny can do the seedlings this once."

As soon as they had given Datt and Levi their dinner, Annie tied up three jars of strawberry jam in a dish towel and hurried barefoot along the road to Amos's farm. She passed the field where Datt and Levi were working, shorthanded today without Gideon and too busy to notice her, and cut across Reuben Beiler's field. It was a long walk, and the sun was hot. Tiny insects flitted around her face, and perspiration made her dress cling to her back.

Annie found Barbara rocking on her shady porch, a pile of mending at her feet and Davy asleep in a cradle beside her.

Barbara jumped up and gave Annie a hug. "How nice to have a visit from you! I'll get you some cold buttermilk, and we'll have a good talk."

"Mamm sent you some strawberry jam," Annie said, immediately feeling at ease here. "We put it up this morning. It looks like we'll be doing another batch tomorrow, there's so many strawberries this year."

"We just eat ours," Barbara said. "Strawberry soup or strawberry shortcake with cream, every night for supper." Barbara laughed. "I hardly cook at all this time of year."

"Amos likes that?" Annie said. "Datt would be in a temper if Mamm served him nothing but strawberries."

"Sure, Amos likes it." She came back with a glass of buttermilk for each of them and settled into her rocker. "Now, Annie, sit down and tell me why you really came."

Annie sagged onto the wooden bench. "Gideon left this morning to take Isaac and the wagon home."

"Yes, Amos told me the wagon looked good when they finished up with it the other night. When do you expect Gideon home again?"

Annie still felt like crying, but the tears seemed to have dried up. "I don't. He's gone for good, Barbara."

Barbara bit off a piece of thread and leaned toward her. "Are you sure? How do you know?"

"He told me. He promised Datt he'd buy tools and come back out on the trolley—Datt gave him permission for that. But he came to my room and told me he's leaving. He's going to Big Valley, to Aaron's. He's taking the train to Lewistown."

"*Ach!*" Barbara exclaimed. "Does anyone else know? Mamm or Levi?"

Annie shook her head.

Barbara drummed her fingers on the arm of the rocker and gazed thoughtfully at her sleeping baby. "It might not be such a terrible thing, Gideon going away. I know this is hard for you to understand, but maybe it will go better for him with

Aaron. Amos has told me Gideon and your Datt don't get along. Amos puts it down to stubbornness on both sides, but I think it's more than that."

"What is it, then?"

"Well, your Datt is always calling Gideon *dopplig*, his mind off someplace else, like that's a bad thing. But my own Datt, he's kind of *dopplig* too. It gets men into trouble sometimes, when they think too much, have other things on their minds, ask too many questions. That's my Datt! Samuel King is always asking questions about the world, wondering why things have to be a certain way with our people. I guess I'm a little bit that way, too," Barbara said with a mischievous smile.

"That's what my Datt says," Annie agreed. " 'Barbara wonders too much,' he says. Datt doesn't believe people should ask questions. It leads them away from their faith and away from God."

"Sometimes it leads them closer," Barbara said. "I wish I could have talked to Gideon before he left. He has to find out certain things about himself. Then maybe someday he can come home again. We'll all miss him, of course, but it might be good for him to spend a few years with your uncle in Big Valley. Meantime you will write to each other and perhaps you can even go out for a visit now and again."

Annie stared at her. How could Barbara think such a thing was possible? "No, we can't. Datt won't allow it. The elders will put Gideon under the *Meidung,* and we'll all have to shun him. That means no letters, no visits, never!"

Barbara leaned over and took Annie's hand. "You may say I'm *dopplig,* but I don't think so. Gideon hasn't been baptized yet, and neither have you, so the elders cannot enforce the *Meidung* against either of you. Here's something to think about: my Datt says, and I believe he's right, that the *Meidung* does no good. What we must do instead is to love the fallen one, the one who has taken a step away. Shunning just drives people further away; it's loving that draws them back."

"But Datt——" Annie began.

Barbara interrupted. "Let's not think about your Datt right now. Let's think about Gideon. Do you know where he is now and when he plans to take the train?"

"They left this morning after breakfast. That's all I know."

Barbara rocked in silence, her fingers to her lips. Davy woke up and began to cry fretfully, and Barbara picked him up and patted him gently. "I've been thinking," she said as she rocked the fussy baby. "I need to make a trip to Lancaster City myself. There's a woman who sells remedies at the market, and she has the best syrup for colic. I could use some for Davy. Now if we were to take our buggy and leave tomorrow early, we could be in Lancaster well before noontime—that gives us plenty of time to go to the market and do some other shopping as well. And maybe, if we ask some questions— I'm good at asking questions!—we can find your friend Isaac. And then, if our luck is good, Isaac can take us to Gideon. It would give you a chance to tell Gideon you'll write to him, and that he's to write to you. He can send the letters to our place. I'll see to it you get them."

"You want me to go with you?" Annie stammered. She had hoped Barbara would have some advice to offer, but she hadn't really expected anything like this. "To the city? But I don't see how——"

"Sure, I mean you! If your Mamm will allow it, of course. We'll stay the night with my sister, Margaret, on Greenfield Road and come home Saturday forenoon."

"It's not Mamm, it's Datt," Annie murmured.

"I know. But we have to think of a way to get around him. It's a first step to having Gideon come home again some day."

Finally they devised a plan and Annie rushed home. Two thoughts jostled for space in her head: The first was *I'm going to see Gideon again!* But the second, darker thought was this: *The first duty of every child is to obey his parents.* That had been taught to her, to all of them since they were toddlers, gently, firmly, and without exception. *The disobedient child is breaking not only his parents' rules but God's.*

Annie had always believed that, never questioning it until now. She knew that Datt would certainly forbid her to see Gideon and to write to him. But she was not certain that God would agree with Datt on everything.

While Isaac and his father settled Goldie in her old home, Gideon perched uneasily in the sitting room with Isaac's mother, who addressed him in a steady stream of her language as she rocked the new baby. Gideon was beginning to see how hard it must have been for Isaac when his family talked Dutch and he probably caught only about half of it. He made out that Isaac's mother was inviting him to spend the night, and he struggled to explain to her, first in English and then in Dutch, that he could not stay. He must buy tools for his father and then be on his way. He was expected, he explained, without saying where or by whom. At last Isaac arrived and straightened things out.

"Stay, Gideon," Isaac said in English, after he had translated for his mother. "At least for supper. They'll be awful disappointed if you don't. Mameh regrets that you've come on a Thursday, because on the night before the Sabbath our suppers are usually just a bowl of cabbage or potato soup, and she would have enjoyed serving you something finer. But plans are being made, and they want you to stay. I do, too."

"All right," Gideon said, because he didn't know how to refuse.

Sarah, Isaac's older sister, was bustling around in the kitchen, and the younger girls went out with a shopping basket. The baby awoke and began to cry, and his mother carried him into the bedroom to nurse him. That left Isaac and Gideon with the peddler, who could not seem to stop asking questions. Suddenly Jakob leaped up. "I must go to see the wagon and Goldie again," he said. "I cannot believe what has happened!"

So they walked down the block to the shed and went over everything for a second and a third time. Isaac and Gideon took turns retelling—Gideon in English, which Isaac translated into Yiddish for Jakob—the story of the day the neighbors had all pitched in to help, adding more details, explaining how each repair had been made and who had made it. Now each item of merchandise was unpacked again, reexamined, exclaimed over again, and repacked. Peddler Jakob wiped tears of joy from his eyes. But when he came to the last box, he pulled out a suit of clothes—trousers, jacket, shirt—somehow missed the last time. "What is this?" he asked.

"They're mine," Gideon stammered, embarrassed. "I forgot they were there. Here, I'll take them." He tucked the bundle under his arm.

When they returned to the house, delicious smells were drifting from the kitchen. A cloth had been spread on the table. Gideon noticed that Sarah had changed into a clean white blouse with lace on the collar and tied a white ribbon in her hair. *How pretty she is,* Gideon thought and looked shyly away.

"A celebration," said the peddler's wife. "In honor of your return, Isaac, and in honor of the friend who has shown us so much kindness." She beamed at Gideon.

The main dish was stuffed cabbage, Isaac explained, and there were meat turnovers and potatoes baked in a flaky crust bought from the bakery—Mameh always made her own, but these were unusual circumstances—and a sponge cake for dessert. Except for the sponge cake, which his own Mawmy often baked, it was all new to Gideon. Still, he liked it. When seconds were offered, Gideon accepted; thirds, too.

Once they had eaten, Isaac's mother again insisted, through Isaac, that Gideon must stay the night, arguing reasonably that it was now much too late to consider taking a trolley all the way back out to the country. She was not certain, of course, she said sweetly, but it seemed unlikely that the trolleys were even running at this hour, and she would feel responsible for another mother's son if something were to happen to Gideon on his way home. It would be a poor way to show gratitude.

"It would honor us if you would stay with us," Peddler Jakob said.

Gideon had seen how small the house was, much smaller than his own home where there were always extra beds for guests. But finally he relented. It was too late to get the tools today anyway. "I'll sleep in the shed with Goldie," he said.

This produced a flurry of protests. Then Isaac, who was surely anxious to spend the night in his own bed again, nevertheless offered, "I will stay out there with him. It is the best thing, Mameh."

It was agreed, then: Isaac and Gideon could spend the night in the shed, if they wished. Soon after sundown but before darkness had settled around them, Isaac and Gideon bid everyone good night and carried a lantern and two bedrolls to the shed. Isaac spread out their blankets on a pile of clean straw. Gideon unpacked his *englische* clothes, laid them out on the wagon seat, and inspected them. He found a pocket mirror in one of the peddler's boxes, tried on the cloth cap, and examined himself in the mirror. He took off the cap.

"I have a favor to ask you," Gideon said. "Cut my hair."

"Cut your hair? But I don't know how to cut hair, Gideon!" Isaac protested. "Mameh always cuts ours."

"It doesn't have to be perfect. Just make it *short*, that's all. Everybody will see my hair and know I'm Amish, even with *englische* clothes. There's scissors in one of the wooden boxes."

"I'll make a mess of it," Isaac warned.

"Doesn't matter. I don't care how it looks, as long as it doesn't look Amish." Gideon found scissors and a comb and sat down on a bale of hay.

"I don't even know where to start," Isaac grumbled.

"Never mind," Gideon said, propping the little mirror on a cobwebbed windowsill. "I'll do it myself."

Gideon grabbed a handful of the long straw-colored hair that hung down past his left ear and chopped it off. Then, awkwardly, he did the same thing on the right side. One side was an inch shorter than the other. He tried to get the sides even, but the problem got worse, and the hair shorter. Next he held his bangs straight up and cut them off about an inch from his scalp. He stepped back and peered into the mirror.

"How do I look?" Gideon asked. "Do I still look Amish?"

"No," Isaac admitted. "You don't even look quite human."

Gideon ran his hand over the ragged stubble and winced. "My cap will cover it, I guess."

"Give me the scissors a minute." Isaac snipped here and there, without much improvement.

Later they blew out the lantern and stretched out on their blankets. Gideon shut his eyes and folded his hands across his chest and began his nightly prayers: *"Unser Vater,"* he began in German, "Our Father, Who art in Heaven . . ." At the end he added, *"O Herr Gott,* bless my father and mother, my brothers and sisters, especially Annie, and give them the grace to forgive me. Amen."

Gideon was tired, but he was much too uneasy and restless to fall asleep. The night was warm, and no air stirred. The straw rustled as he turned this way and that. Occasionally he reached up to touch his ragged hair.

"You still awake?" Isaac whispered.

"Umhmm."

"Maybe you ought to go to a barber tomorrow."

"Maybe." Gideon shoved a handful of straw under his head for a pillow. "Good night now, Isaac."

"Good night."

CHAPTER 17

"Where's Gideon?" Ben asked at breakfast on Friday.

"Seems like he should be back by now," Datt said. "He should have got there by noon, done the errands I gave him, and been back here by last evening."

"He must have decided to stay over," Levi suggested. "Goldie isn't the fastest horse, and her leg might still be giving her trouble. They probably had to take it slow."

"Better to stay over than come back so late on the trolley," Mamm said, "and then have to walk all the way from the trolley stop."

"Huh," Datt muttered. "I gave him

money for tools—new plane, some files and such. That boy cannot seem to keep his mind on business. I hope he's not up to some foolishness."

"I expect he'll be home in time for dinner," Mamm said.

Annie kept her eyes on her plate. There was so much she had to hold inside: that Gideon would not be back by dinnertime, and that soon she herself would be on her way to Lancaster City with Barbara to search for him.

Barbara and Annie had agreed that Annie was to say nothing to her parents, not even to Mamm. Then sometime after breakfast, when Datt and Levi could be expected to be out in the field, Barbara would arrive as if by chance and invite Annie to accompany her to the city. It was much safer than if Annie asked permission ahead of time. Datt would surely say no, and Mamm, knowing what Datt would say, would naturally say no, too. Annie was counting on Barbara to persuade Mamm to let her go.

It was almost fifteen miles to Central

Market, an hour and a half with one stop to tend to Davy and to rest the buggy horse, but they could still be in Lancaster by nine o'clock and have the whole day to hunt for Gideon and for Barbara to do her errands.

At this moment Barbara was probably trotting along the county road, due to arrive in a few minutes. But to Annie's horror, as Datt pushed back from the table he said, "Annie, I need you to come out and help today. We're shorthanded without Gideon."

Annie groped for something to say. There were so many things that could have gone wrong: Barbara might have changed her mind, or Davy might have been too colicky to be taken on such a long trip. Or Amos could have put his foot down and told Barbara she mustn't go. But Annie had not supposed that Datt would want her to help him in the field, and there was nothing she could say.

Numbly she stood up to go with Datt. She would not even have a chance to tell Barbara herself what had happened.

Barbara would arrive, and Annie would already have gone out to the field. But then Mamm stepped in. "She'll come out a little later, Ezra. I need her to help me here first." Annie was weak with relief.

Datt nodded, and he and Levi took their old straw hats down from the pegs by the kitchen door. As soon as they had left for the barn to harness up the work-horses, Mamm looked at Annie with concern. "Are you feeling all right?" she asked. "You don't look so good. Like you sampled too many strawberries yesterday when we were putting them up."

"I'm all right, Mamm," Annie replied, her mind racing in search of a way out. If she said that she wasn't feeling well, Mamm wouldn't let her go out to the tobacco field, but neither would she let her go to Lancaster with Barbara. Maybe Annie should simply tell Mamm about the trip they had planned—but without mentioning the real purpose. "I feel fine," she said.

"All right, then," Mamm said. "If you're sure."

But then a small miracle occurred. A

gray-topped buggy clattered up the lane and into the barnyard. Amos was driving and Barbara sat next to him with the baby on her lap. "I've come to give Datt a hand, what with Gideon away," Amos said, climbing down.

Mamm was all smiles as she reached out to take her grandson, but Barbara was brisk and businesslike. "I'm going to Lancaster to get some colic remedy for Davy," Barbara said. "I thought I'd stop and visit my sister, Margaret, and her new baby on the way home. We'll stay the night with her and be back tomorrow morning. It's too much of a trip for me to make by myself, but if Annie could come along . . ."

Mamm frowned and considered. "I'm a bit concerned about Annie—her nerves seem kind of unsteady lately." Then she made up her mind. "All right," she said, and Annie let go of the breath she'd been holding. "This trip might be just what she needs. Annie, run upstairs and put on your next-best dress. And don't forget your bonnet."

Annie raced to her room to change her

clothes while Barbara talked to Mamm about the woman who sold herbs and patent remedies at Central Market and Mamm put together a bundle of small gifts to send to Margaret. Annie would never have guessed yesterday morning as she had watched Gideon drive the peddler's wagon through the gate that she would feel so hopeful today. Now there was a chance.

He has to find out certain things about himself, Barbara had said. *It might be good for him to spend a few years with your uncle in Big Valley.*

Surely it won't be that long, Annie thought as she tied her high black shoes. *Maybe after a few weeks or even a month or two he'll decide that he made the wrong choice and be ready to come home.* Datt would be furious, of course. There would be plenty of hollering and maybe even a smacking, but then it would be over. Better to be hollered at and hit a few times, Annie believed, than to be lost forever.

A few minutes later Annie was seated

beside Barbara in the family buggy with Davy on her lap. Barbara clucked at Nickel, the gray gelding, and Danny ran to open the gate. They rolled down the lane, and Nickel settled into a steady pace. They passed the field where the men were working. Barbara waved, and Amos waved back, while Annie sank into the seat, hoping that Datt wouldn't notice her. She felt a little ashamed for sneaking off like this. Then she remembered what Barbara had said: *Shunning just drives people further away; it's loving that draws them back.*

On Friday morning Gideon made his way through the quiet streets toward what he thought must be the center of Lancaster. It seemed late to him, but this place was just waking up. A housewife carrying a bucket and a broom opened her door and commenced scrubbing the bricks in front of her house. Soon all up and down Duke Street women were emerging to scour their few square feet of sidewalk. Gideon dodged the rivers of soapy water flowing into the gutter. *Imagine if that was all the land you had, that little square of bricks,* Gideon thought. He felt sorry for these city people.

Gideon had gotten up before sunrise, washed at a faucet in the alley behind the shed, and quietly dressed in his *englische* clothes, trying not to disturb Isaac. He was struggling to knot the silk necktie when Isaac woke up. "You're up already?" he asked. "Where are you going?"

"To see about Datt's tools," Gideon had told him, shoving the tie in his pocket. "And I forgot to ask you—will you take them to him when you go out next time? Or can you think of some way to get them out there beforehand? I know Datt. When I don't come back, he'll think I was up to some monkey business. I don't want him thinking I took his money."

"But nothing's open yet," Isaac said, yawning. "This is the city, not like the farm where everybody gets up in the dark to milk the cows and goes to bed while it's still daylight. And Mameh will expect you to come in for breakfast."

"I want to be there when the shop opens," Gideon had explained. "Then I have to find some place to sell my book and my mouth organ, to get train fare."

Now, following the network of trolley wires strung overhead, Gideon turned out King Street and headed toward a tall monument in the center of an open square. On all sides of the square, shopkeepers were opening their shutters, preparing for business. Some of the shops were huge, bigger than the biggest barn, taking up the better part of a square block and towering several stories high. Nearby were the twin brick towers of Central Market; Gideon remembered them from the times he'd gone there with his own family.

Gazing in the show window of a shop selling ladies' hats, Gideon caught sight of his own reflection. He scarcely recognized himself in his unfamiliar clothes. He practiced tipping his cloth cap, the way he had seen *Englishers* do it, but when he swept off the cap and saw his butchered hair, he crushed the cap down over his ears as far as it would go.

The first time a gray-topped buggy

trotted smartly along King Street, Gideon ducked into an alley between buildings, afraid someone would recognize him. But then he saw more and more Amish buggies, dozens of them. Many were backed up to the curb, and the women were setting up tables on the sidewalk and arranging mounds of green tomatoes, baskets of strawberries, jars of jam, loaves of bread, pyramids of eggs. Hand-lettered signs listed the prices.

Gideon tilted his cap over his eyes and hurried past them. He knew that many Amish families living close to Lancaster, around Smoketown and Witmer, kept stands at the big market houses or sold their produce out of the back of their buggies. Even if he did see somebody he knew, he decided they wouldn't recognize him—not in these *englische* clothes.

He plunged his hands into the pockets of his pants, in the manner of *Englishers,* and sauntered slowly around the square, taking in the sights. He bought two sticky buns from a woman who looked a lot like Mamm's sister Lena and did his best to talk the way he thought *Englishers* talked. Next he bought a cup of lemonade from a boy about Ben's age. The boy stared at him.

"What are you looking at?" Gideon asked the boy.

"Your hair. It's sure funny-looking."

The boy's mother came over and shushed him and gave Gideon his change. Gideon noticed that she stared too, although she pretended not to.

Gideon finished his breakfast and followed the sound of music to the north corner of the square. A blind old Negro dressed in clothing mended with bright-colored patches was playing an accordion. The man had placed a battered tin cup on the sidewalk in front of him, and people passing by tossed pennies into it. Gideon leaned against a tree and listened to the lively tunes the old man produced by squeezing and pulling the box while his fingers skipped nimbly over the keyboard. Gideon patted the mouth organ he had stuck in his pocket and wished he could play it just half as good as that.

Gideon's friend Crist had traded him the mouth organ for a string of trout the day the two had gone fishing and Gideon had had all the luck. He never did know how Crist came to have a mouth organ, except that Crist always seemed to get hold of interesting things that no one else had. Trouble was, when you had a forbidden treasure, you often got your pleasure only from *having* it, not from using it. There had never been any chance to learn to play the mouth organ.

At least Gideon's other treasure, *Treasure Island,* was silent. Gideon could get it out and look at it on the sly, read the story again, and admire the pictures. Not that the story was easy; the language was at times as difficult for Gideon to make out as the words in Datt's German Bible, and there were parts that he never did quite understand. Even that song the pirates sang—"Fifteen men on the dead man's chest—Yo-ho-ho, and a bottle of rum!"—made little sense to him. But Gideon had taken a real liking to young Jim Hawkins and worried about the boy's fate, never quite sure if he was a real person or a made-up one. What appealed to him was the idea that such other worlds and such things as pirates and buried treasure and ships that sailed far away might have existed.

Gideon reached in his pocket and ran his fingers over the mouth organ's holes. It gave him courage to know that he could pull it out right now if he wanted to and blow on it all he wished. No Datt would step up behind him with a buggy whip and order him to get rid of the worldly thing.

"What you standin' there gawkin' for?" the accordion player asked. If Gideon had not been able to see for himself that the musician's eyes were milky and sightless, he would have believed the man was looking right at him.

"Just listening," Gideon said. "I like your music."

"You don' have a penny shows how much you like it?"

"No," he admitted. "I have three dollars less a dime."

"You Amish, right?"

"How did you know that?"

The Negro merely chuckled and squeezed out a few bouncy chords. "And I bet you got on English clothes, right again?"

"I thought you were blind," Gideon said nervously.

"That I am, that I am. But I can hear real good. And I can hear that you talk English like an Amishman. And if you're surprised by that, and you did sound surprised, it means you got on clothes don't b'long to you. Here's something else: if you got on regular clothes, that means you're trying to look regular because you're running away." The musician's thick fingers rambled up and down the keyboard, picking out a cheerful melody.

The way the man figured things out was scary, but Gideon plucked up his courage. "It's more like I'm going for a visit. I'm on my way to my uncle's in Big Valley, after I get my Datt's tools for him. And I have to get money for my train fare. I don't suppose you know where I could sell a mouth organ, do you?"

"Lemme see it."

Gideon handed over the mouth organ. The blind man delicately fingered the silvery metal etched with a flowery design. He cupped the instrument to his mouth and coaxed from it a sad, sweet melody. Gideon and Crist had tried this a few times. They blew and sucked air through it. Gideon liked the tones he produced, but he didn't know how to go about making a real tune. The blind musician did.

"I'll give you a dollar for it," the man said finally.

"All right."

The blind man fumbled in his pants pocket and came up with a handful of change—two quarters, three dimes, three nickels, five pennies. "Now you got a penny to put in my cup," he said, chuckling.

Gideon's penny clinked in the tin cup, and he put the rest of the money into his own pocket.

"Blind Johnny Shindle thanks you," the man said, "and may God bless and keep you. Got anything else you want to sell me?"

"I have a book here," Gideon said. "It's called *Treasure Island.*"

The musician played three notes on the accordion. "Three blind mice," he sang. "See how they run." Then he laughed. "Afraid I can't help you there, sonny," he said. "I'm a poor customer for books."

Embarrassed, Gideon dropped another penny in the tin cup and hurried away. "They all ran after the farmer's wife," Blind Johnny sang. "She cut off their tails with a carving knife. Did you ever see such a sight . . ."

The sound of the quick, merry tune followed Gideon all the way up the street, toward the towers of Central Market.

The minute Isaac entered the house for breakfast, his sisters gathered around him, wanting to know all about Gideon; Sarah was especially curious. "He is very handsome," she sighed, and Isaac wondered if she'd still think so when she saw what had become of his hair. Mameh could not understand how a young man could go off without any breakfast. Tateh wanted another opportunity to thank Gideon.

"He will be back before he leaves . . ." Isaac almost said "for Big Valley" but caught himself and then could not think of how to explain how he would be back. Gideon had left his Amish clothes in a bundle in the shed, and he'd told Isaac he wanted to take them along. But the main reason he was coming back was to leave his Datt's tools for Peddler Jakob to deliver on his next trip to the Stoltzfus farm. How would Gideon explain why he wasn't taking them along on the trolley he was supposedly catching this afternoon? Worst of all were the English clothes and the dreadful haircut. What would Mameh and Tateh think about that?

But Isaac had little time to worry about explanations for Gideon's behavior. Word had gotten out that Isaac was back with Goldie and the wagon. Abie Siegel escaped from the clutches of the *melamed* around noon, since *cheder* ended early on

Fridays for the start of the Sabbath. Almost immediately he had appeared at Isaac's house.

"Tell, tell, tell!" Abie ordered, scarcely out of hearing of Isaac's family. "What was it like, living with those *goyim*? Did you eat *treyf*? Ha, I'll bet you did! Was it good? Like I told you? No lies, now."

"Come on, let's go see the wagon," Isaac said, edging Abie away from the house. Joshua was crying and Mameh was lying down to rest. "It's all fixed up. I'll show you."

But while Isaac was trying to show off the wagon he had helped paint, Abie, who had eyes like an eagle, spotted the pile of blond hair on the floor of the stable. "Hey! What's all this?" he asked. And next he found the neatly rolled bundle of Amish clothing tucked next to a folded blanket.

So Isaac had to tell him the whole long story—of the Stoltzfus family and his friend Annie and her brother Gideon who didn't get along with his Datt and had decided to leave and was now wandering somewhere around Lancaster. It was, Isaac realized, a complicated tale.

"Whew." Abie whistled when Isaac had finished. "And I thought only Jews had troubles."

CHAPTER 18

Where do we start looking?" Annie asked Barbara uneasily.

At first the trip had seemed exciting, especially after Barbara and Annie had left behind the farms with which Annie was familiar. But Davy had been cranky all morning and they'd had to stop twice so that Barbara could nurse him and change his diaper. And although Barbara was brave and determined, she didn't have much experience driving a buggy in the middle of a city with clanging trolleys, wagons and buggies, crowds of people on the street, *and* a crying baby beside her. Annie and Barbara were both hot and tired, as well as anxious. How would they ever find Gideon in this big city?

"First, we'll look for the railroad station," Barbara decided, "and find out when the train leaves, so we're sure not to miss him. Then we'll go to the market. I'll get the colic syrup and maybe that will help Davy."

True to her word, Barbara seemed fearless about asking questions. Soon she found her way to the railroad station and hitched Nickel to a post outside. In wonderment Annie gazed around the vast echoing building with a high domed ceiling and marble floors. But Barbara headed straight to the cage where tickets were sold.

"When is the next train to Lewistown?" she asked.

The ticket seller consulted a schedule. "Two-nineteen," he said gruffly.

Barbara studied the huge clock high up on the wall. "It's ten of ten. Good," she said to Annie. "We have time."

Finding Central Market was simple enough; the twin brick towers were visible from a considerable distance. Annie trailed after Barbara, past row after row of stalls where farmers' wives sold eggs by the dozen, bushels of vegetables, wheels of cheese, and chickens and turkeys dressed and ready for the oven; butchers in bloody aprons hacked at sides of beef hanging from hooks; fishmongers presented oysters fresh from Chesapeake Bay. The times that Annie had been here with Datt and Mamm she had felt overwhelmed by the hugeness of the place, the bustle and din of people buying and selling; this time was no different.

Finally they reached a small section of household items, washboards and kerosene and stove blacking. It was here that Barbara found Irma Baumgarten and her tiny booth stocked with medicinal herbs and remedies. It took only a few moments to explain the problem to Irma and a few moments more for Irma to recommend the proper treatment. She popped a spoonful of dark brown syrup into Davy's mouth. Before Barbara had counted out the coins and Irma had filled a medicine bottle from her large container, Davy had already stopped fussing.

On the way out Barbara paused long enough to buy a chunk of Lebanon bologna and a wedge of white cheddar to take home to Amos as a special treat. Then she thought perhaps she should pick up a few little things for her sister, Margaret, and Margaret's new baby. A bottle of the miracle colic remedy might also be a good thing to take Margaret, Barbara decided. So back they went to Irma Baumgarten's booth for a second bottle of the brown syrup. While she was there, Barbara let herself be sold a new kind of tea said to be good for a variety of complaints. Annie thought they would never leave, that surely they would miss the chance to intercept Gideon before he got on the train.

But they arrived back at the railroad station with over an hour to spare. Barbara inquired where the train would leave from, and they found a bench where they could watch Track Two and everybody who came to board that train.

The hands of the clock inched toward two o'clock. Still there was no sign of Gideon. Then a loud voice announced the arrival on Track Two of the train from Philadelphia, bound for Harrisburg, Lewistown, Altoona, Johnstown, and Pittsburgh. They felt, and then heard, the rumble of the train, and a crowd of people surged toward the gate to Track Two. Gideon was nowhere to be seen.

Minutes later the conductor called, "All aboard!" No Gideon.

The whistle blew once, twice; steam snorted from the engine; then the great train began to move, and the stationmaster closed the metal gate. Gideon had not boarded that train.

Then a terrible thought struck Annie: *What if there was an earlier train?* "Barbara," Annie ventured, "is that the only train? Or are there others? I was just thinking . . ."

"Oh my!" Barbara exclaimed. "Well, let's go find out."

Barbara stepped up to the ticket booth again and was told that two trains a day stopped in Lewistown: the 8:32 A.M. and the 2:19 P.M.

The two stared at each other. "Oh,

Barbara!" Annie wailed. "What if he took the early train!"

Both of them burst into tears, right in the middle of the station. Davy woke up and started crying again.

Barbara was the first to recover. She pulled out a handkerchief, dabbed at her eyes, and passed the handkerchief to Annie. "Maybe we didn't miss him. Maybe he didn't get on the morning train after all. It's possible. It could be that Gideon is still in Lancaster. What we have to do now is find Isaac. He's sure to know where Gideon is."

Barbara drove Nickel uneasily through a part of the city she had not visited before. Both Annie and Barbara were tired and dispirited. After the disappointment of the missed train and the fears that they might have missed Gideon after all, they had sat in the buggy and while Davy slept they had eaten some of the Lebanon bologna and cheese that Barbara had bought for Amos.

Then Barbara had asked another of the

many questions she had had to ask that day: directions to the part of town where the Jews lived. The narrow streets were even more crowded than the streets around the market, but Barbara's was the only Amish buggy. A few people looked at them, as though surprised to see them there, but most people on the street simply ignored them.

Now Barbara stared at Annie in disbelief. "You mean that Isaac stayed with your family for almost two weeks and you don't know his last name?"

"I never asked," Annie said simply.

"It was on that letter I brought for him!" Barbara recalled suddenly. "But I can't remember it. Try to think, Annie. You saw that letter, too. Do you remember the name?"

"I think it started with an *L*."

"Let's keep thinking." Barbara leaned out of the buggy and spoke to a man who stood on the curb, sharpening scissors and knives in the back of a small cart. "I'm looking for a peddler named Jakob," she said. "Medium height with a bushy black beard."

The scissor-grinder laughed. "Half the people in this neighborhood look like that," he said. "And the other half are women. Take half the men and they'll turn out to be peddlers. Lots of them are named Jakob."

They quickly found out again what Annie already knew: their language was similar but different from what the Jews spoke. Many of the people Barbara talked to couldn't seem to understand her, whether she spoke to them in Dutch or in English. And Barbara couldn't make out much of what they said to her.

"We'll just drive around until we find them," Barbara announced. But as the afternoon wore on, they had no luck. Then Davy was awake and cranky again, and they needed to find a place for Barbara to nurse him.

"What do we do now?" Annie asked dejectedly. It seemed that their wonderful plan was not going to work after all.

"Try again tomorrow. We'll go to Margaret's and spend the night. We'll come back into the city bright and early and go straight to the railroad station. If

Gideon comes to catch the eight-thirty-two train to Lewistown, we're sure to find him. If not, well, we'll try again to find Isaac's family and ask about Gideon. And if Gideon's already gone, then I guess we just have to go home. They'll worry if we don't."

"But I'll still write to him," Annie said. She felt exhausted and defeated.

"Yes, Annie. You'll still write to him. And one day you'll see him again, I can almost promise you that."

The sun was setting behind the steep roofs of Lancaster City as Barbara and Annie set off again, this time on the road to Witmer.

Nothing had gone quite as Gideon hoped. First there had been the problem of finding a shop that sold the tools Datt wanted. Then, although Gideon shopped carefully, the tools cost more than the three dollars—minus the dime for breakfast—Datt had given him. Gideon had to make up the difference from the dollar—minus two pennies for Blind

Johnny's tin cup—he had gotten for the mouth organ.

Finally he hurried to the railroad station to inquire about the next train that would stop at Lewistown and the price of a ticket.

"One way or round-trip?" asked the man at the ticket counter, peering at him curiously.

Gideon hesitated for only a second. "One way."

"One dollar and eighty cents. The next train leaves at two-nineteen, Track Two. That's two hours and ten minutes from now." The ticket seller peered at Gideon with arched eyebrows, ready to hand over a ticket. But Gideon shook his head. He didn't need to count his coins to know that he was eighty-six cents short of the price of a ticket. Furthermore he was hungry, and a bite of dinner would use up some of what little he did have left.

"And the one after that?"

"Leaves eight-thirty-two tomorrow morning."

Gideon turned and left the station, sure

the ticket seller was secretly laughing at him. In fact it seemed to him that everywhere he went people were secretly laughing at him. They probably all knew, just as Blind Johnny Shindle did, that he was an Amishman with an awful haircut, dressed up in *englische* clothes, and not fooling anybody. Those who weren't laughing at him were Amish people, and he suspected that they were ashamed for him, or at least disapproving.

Gideon purchased a soda pop and two frankfurters on buns from a street vendor and sat down on a bench to eat his dinner with the bundle of his father's tools beside him. Across from the bench a large clock stood on a corner outside a department store. Gideon watched the minute hand creep slowly past the half hour and tried to think what to do next. The minutes ticked by. Still Gideon could not figure out a way to get enough money together for the train fare. He was down now to seventy-eight cents, short a dollar and two cents. He still had his precious copy of *Treasure Island,* but how was he to go about selling it?

Gideon opened the book and carefully examined the map on the first page, admiring again the drawing of the buccaneer. He turned the page and read the description: "a tall, strong, heavy, nut-brown man; his tarry pigtail falling over the shoulders of his soiled blue coat; his hands ragged and scarred, with black, broken nails; and the sabre cut across one cheek, a dirty, livid white."

The clock on the corner struck one. There was scarcely time to sell the book, find his way back to Isaac's house, leave the tools, collect his Amish clothes, and hurry to the station in time to buy a ticket and climb aboard the 2:19.

Gideon shrugged and continued reading. It was the first time since he left school that he had sat down when he pleased to read what he pleased. Time passed swiftly. He barely noticed when two o'clock struck, but when it rang the half hour Gideon reluctantly closed the book.

For a while Gideon walked aimlessly, up one street and down the next, the book and the bundle with Datt's tools under his arm. Once he even thought of returning the tools to the store where he had bought them and asking for the money back; he would have enough for train fare then, and he could repay Datt at a later time. But he dismissed that idea as dishonest. The money would weigh on his conscience.

Then he got the idea of asking Peddler Jakob for advice. Jakob was a salesman, and surely he would know where and how this book could be sold. Jakob would ask questions, of course, and Gideon would have to explain why he had not gone home on the trolley, why he had cut his hair, why he needed to sell the book. But Gideon felt that Jakob would understand; he had once left home himself.

Late in the afternoon, hot, dusty, and thirsty, Gideon headed back to the part of town where Isaac's family lived. The streets that had been so quiet this morning were lively: men with full beards dressed in long black coats and black hats conversed on street corners, women in dark shawls hurried along with shopping baskets. Gideon felt as though he stuck out in this crowd in his peculiar clothes even more than among the *Englishers,* and he threaded his way through alleys to the shed where Goldie was kept. The horse had already been fed and watered, he noticed, and her stall was clean and spread with fresh straw.

Gideon peeled off the uncomfortable pants and shirt and washed up at the outside faucet. His own Amish clothes still lay in the corner, and he slipped them on with relief. Then he put on his plain black hat, half hoping that his chopped-off hair would escape the notice of Isaac's family. *Perhaps I should wait awhile,* Gideon thought, *and not interrupt their supper.* He sat down on a bale of hay and read another chapter of *Treasure Island.*

When he felt he had waited long enough and could face Isaac's family, Gideon walked down the block to their house. The sun was setting and a breeze stirred the leaves, although the brick sidewalks still shimmered with heat. He expected to find the girls playing on the sidewalk, as they had been when they arrived yesterday, but somehow it was all different. The streets were suddenly quiet; everyone seemed to have disappeared. Shyly Gideon knocked at the door.

A moment later Sarah appeared. Again she was wearing the white blouse with lace on the collar, but now she had added a tiny gold pin at the throat and the ribbon in her dark hair was pink. Amish girls were not allowed to wear lace or hair ribbons or jewelry, but Gideon thought these signs of worldliness made Sarah even more beautiful. Sarah smiled at him and Gideon grinned back.

"Hello, Gideon," she said. "I thought you had gone back to the farm, but I see that you're still here." She stepped back from the screen door. "Please come in."

Gideon pulled open the door and stepped inside, unprepared for the scene that greeted him. Everyone in Isaac's family was dressed up in their good clothes, and Peddler Jakob had a white silk shawl of some kind draped around his shoulders.

A fresh white linen cloth was spread on the table where they had eaten supper the previous evening. On the cloth were arranged two plump golden loaves of braided bread, a pair of candlesticks, and a silver cup. Gideon stopped, feeling foolish, and fumbled for something to say.

But Peddler Jakob sprang forward and embraced him and began talking to him in their language. "You're just in time for the Sabbath," Isaac explained. "Welcome, Gideon."

CHAPTER 19

Tell them the whole story," Isaac advised Gideon. "I'll translate for you. They'll understand. And maybe then we'll be able to think of a way to help you."

It had not been easy for Isaac to convince Gideon that he needed to tell Mameh and Tateh everything: why he had decided to leave, where he was going, why he had left without informing his parents. "And you'll have to explain why you cut your hair," Isaac insisted. "That's part of the story, too."

Gideon's arrival moments before Mameh lit the candles and ushered in the Sabbath had been a complete surprise. Isaac could not remember ever having such an unusual guest for their Friday night observance, and he was pleased to have his friend there. Tateh was his usual exuberant self, welcoming Gideon and proclaiming it "a double feast—no, no, triple! Not only do we welcome Queen Sabbath into our home but also the return of our precious son, and now, most joyfully, his kind friend!"

And for the second night in a row Sarah had prepared, under Mameh's direction, a wonderful meal. Mameh was feeling much better, much stronger today—"Because my darling son has returned," she said—and she had helped to prepare an especially festive meal. Instead of the customary chicken, Sarah had carefully cooked a brisket of beef, the tenderest, most flavorful dish Isaac could imagine. The red beet eggs had been dutifully examined and sampled at lunch and even somewhat enjoyed by Tirzah and Leah, who had not been compelled to eat them at nearly every meal for days on end. But they made no appearance at this meal.

Isaac was glad to see how much Gideon enjoyed the food. "But now you must explain what's happening," Isaac said.

As Gideon's story unfolded, Mameh

and Tateh listened intently. Sometimes they asked questions in Yiddish that Isaac then translated. As Isaac had hoped, they were sympathetic. When Gideon finished, Tateh cleared his throat.

"There are two problems, then, as I understand it. First, we must get word to your parents so they do not worry themselves too much about you. It wounds a parent deeply when a son is absent, I can assure you of that. I will undertake to do that for you when I deliver your father's tools to him next week. Isaac and I will leave on Monday on that errand."

Isaac grinned with pleasure when he heard that; he had not been expecting to be allowed to go out with Tateh again— at least not this soon.

Gideon nodded. "You're very kind," he said.

Tateh shook his head. "We owe your parents a deep debt of gratitude. This is a way in which we can begin to repay it." Tateh took a sip of tea from his glass. "Now the second problem is that you intend to leave on the westbound train tomorrow morning, is that right? But you do not have sufficient fare for the ticket."

"All I have," Gideon said, "is this book, *Treasure Island.* I was hoping to sell it. I sold my mouth organ to a musician on the square for a dollar, but some of that I spent on the tools. And some," he added, "for two frankfurters and a soda pop."

"And how much money do you need?"

"A dollar and two cents. I believe the book is worth a dollar." He laid the book on the table. "I don't know about the extra pennies."

Tateh gazed at the book. "I have no doubt," he said, "that your handsome book is worth at least a dollar and two cents. And I would be pleased to purchase it from you for that amount. The difficulty is, Gideon, that the Sabbath has begun. It began at sunset this evening, and it will end at sunset tomorrow. During this time, I as a devout Jew am not permitted to transact any business."

"I understand," Gideon said, after Isaac had explained what Tateh had said. "We have the same rule. No business on the Sabbath."

Sarah had been watching and listening silently all this time. Isaac had observed that she gazed intently at Gideon whenever he was looking at someone else in the family, but as soon as his eyes met hers, she immediately looked away. Now she left the table, examined the cups into which Mameh sorted the coins Tateh brought from his trips, and returned to murmur softly, "The *pushke*, Tateh. The cup for charity."

"I do not understand, my daughter. What do you mean?"

"You cannot do business on the Sabbath. But you can offer charity, can you not? Perhaps Gideon can look into the *pushke* and find a dollar and two cents there. And when he goes to the train tomorrow, perhaps he can leave his book here, as a gift for Isaac. I have a little money saved. I can replenish the *pushke* when the Sabbath is over."

"Excellent, my daughter!"

Gideon looked curiously from Sarah to Tateh and then at Isaac. "What's she saying?"

Isaac explained, and Gideon beamed and slapped his knee. "Your sister would make a fine Amish woman," he said. "She's like my brother Amos's wife, Barbara, who is good at finding a way around the rules."

Sarah, Isaac noticed, blushed deeply.

That night Gideon was given a bedroll and a lantern—he had to light it himself, since Isaac's family could not make a fire on the Sabbath—and allowed to sleep in the stable again.

"Please come back tomorrow morning," Mameh said, "and help yourself to food for the journey. No need to spend money for food. There is plenty here."

Isaac walked with Gideon to the stable. "I think my sister likes you," he said.

"Yes," Gideon said with a smile. "I like her, too."

* * *

"Litsky," Annie said as she stumbled out of bed Saturday morning before sunup.

Barbara propped herself on an elbow and looked over at Annie. "You remembered."

"During the night. I woke up and there it was. I could see it plain as day on the envelope: *Isaac Litsky.*"

Barbara sat up wearily. "I'm surprised you could think of anything. Babies crying all night long!" She leaned over the cradle where Davy was howling again. "What makes you so miserable, my little one?" she crooned and scooped him up. "*Ach, what is this?*"

Annie looked. Davy seemed to be covered all over with tiny red spots. Together they rushed off to seek the advice of Margaret, who had recently given birth to her fifth child.

"Chicken pox," Margaret said after a brisk examination. "Poor little thing. You're not planning to go back into the city today, surely?"

"Of course not," Barbara said, cuddling the wailing baby.

Annie felt the world drop out from under her.

Barbara turned to her. "Annie, there's no reason you can't go and look for Gideon yourself."

"Oh no! I couldn't!" Annie protested.

"Of course you can. And you will. And then, when you've found him and seen him off with love and promised to answer the letters he's going to write you, you can come back here and pick us up and we'll go home, if Davy's well enough."

And so Annie found herself driving Amos's buggy right through the middle of Lancaster, her hands sweating with nervousness. Barbara was right: she *could* remember the streets, just as she remembered Isaac's last name, and Nickel *would* follow her clucks and tugs on the rein, and she *would* find the railroad station in time.

Then, here was Annie, stepping boldly up to the ticket master's cage to inquire from which track the 8:32 would depart for Lewistown.

And here was Annie, running heedlessly across the polished marble floor and planting herself breathlessly in front of a startled Gideon.

"Annie!" he exclaimed, his mouth open and his eyes wide.

Annie was so happy to see Gideon that she almost didn't notice his hair. He was wearing Amish clothes, not that terrible *englische* outfit, but his hair . . .

Gideon pulled on his nose, the way he did when he was embarrassed. "A mistake," he said. "But it will grow. Now," he said in a firmer voice, "tell me what you're doing here. Who brought you? Datt isn't looking for me, is he?"

Annie shook her head. "Barbara and I came yesterday. We looked everywhere for you, Gideon!" She told Gideon where they had been, what they had done, about the night in Witmer. "Davy's come down with chicken pox," she explained. "And Barbara said I must come by myself to see you off, and I did!"

Gideon looked at Annie, shaking his head. "I can't believe it. I just can't believe it," he said, over and over. "First, let me buy my ticket, and then we can sit down for a minute. The train won't be

here for a while. I want to look at you—
my grown-up sister! And I want you to
tell me why you made this long trip."

"To see you," Annie said. While they
stood in the line waiting to buy Gideon's
ticket, Annie told him every detail she
could think of about her journey here and
begged him for details of his own journey.

"Will you get home all right?" Gideon
asked. "You're such a brave girl!"

"Of course I will," Annie protested,
pleased that he was proud of her. But the
line moved slowly, and before there was
time for Annie to say all the things that
were in her heart, she felt the rumble of
the train coming into the station. Then
came the announcement of the departure
of the 8:32 for Harrisburg, Lewistown,
Altoona . . .

Gideon stood up. "It's time to go,
Annie."

Oddly enough, Annie didn't feel like
crying. "I'll write to you, Gideon," she
said, "if you'll write to me."

That look of surprise crossed his face
again. "You know Datt won't allow it. I'll
be under the *Meidung*."

"I don't care," Annie said. She stuck her chin out. "Barbara says you can write to me at their place."

"Maybe it would be better at Isaac's," Gideon said. "That way it won't put Amos in a bad way, and Barbara, too."

"Barbara doesn't mind."

"Still." Gideon rummaged in his pocket and pulled out a scrap of paper.

"All aboooard!" the conductor cried.

"This is Aaron's address. I'll write you as soon as I can. I already sent a letter to Mamm and Datt saying where I went." Steam belched from the locomotive. Gideon started to run.

"Good-bye, Annie!" he called.

"Good-bye, Gideon!" Annie called back. She watched her brother swing aboard the last car just as the great train jerked and began to move.

Gideon stood on the car platform, waving and waving as the train pulled out. Annie waved until his black Amish hat was a speck in the distance. She was certain now that she'd see him again. Loving would draw him back.

CHAPTER **20**

2nd July 1911

Dear Isaac,

Well here I am in Big Valley. It's a pretty place all right with plenty of good farming. You will never guess who showed up at the train station Saturday morning to see me off. My sister Annie. Her and Amos's wife Barbara went to visit relatives in Witmer and Annie came all by herself to find me at the train. She told me she will write to me and I promised to write to her. But as I explained to you Datt will not allow it. So I am writing to ask you to do another favor for me. Please take the letter I am enclosing and see she gets it but without Datt finding out. I don't want to get her in trouble. His eyes would pop right out of his head if he knew.

More later. Regards to your folks and tell your sister Sarah hello from me.

Your friend,
Gideon

2nd July 1911

Dear Annie,

Greetings from Big Valley, Belleville, Mifflin County, Pennsylvania. I am finally here.

I liked riding on the train. You will, too, when you come here to visit. But don't do what I did and arrive without notice. When Aaron said they live a good piece out from town I didn't know he meant almost as far as from our farm to Lancaster City. I got off the train without the least idea of where to go or what to do but I was in luck. There was an Amishman at the train depot to pick up someone else and he gave me a ride all the way out to Big Valley to Aaron's place. Were they surprised when I walked in the door just in time for supper. Lydia is a good cook but not as good as Mamm.

We are starting to cut hay and it's just as much work here as it is where you are. And Aaron hollers as much as Datt. Still it's working out good.

I miss you a lot, Annie, Mamm and the others too, even Datt, but mostly you. I look forward to your letter.

Your brother,
Gideon

P.S. My hair is growing out but even Aaron was shocked.

15th of July

Dear Gideon,

Isaac brought me your letter. I will keep it and all other letters you send in the future in your old hidey-hole.

As you can imagine I was plenty worried about what was going to happen after seeing you off at the train. Davy was still sick when I got to Barbara's sister's place but we decided to hurry home and were there by dinnertime. Mamm was so upset that you still weren't back, and it was hard for me not to tell her I knew where you were. Then your letter came, and what a black day that was. As expected, no one is allowed to mention your name in our house. When I want to talk about you, I have to think of an excuse to run over to Barbara's. How your ears must ring when we're together! Everybody has a different idea about it. According to Barbara, Amos believes you did the right thing by going but he can't come out and say so. Levi is like Datt. Ben and Danny are upset but afraid to ask. Katie asks where you are, and Mamm says "Gone away" and cries some more. I saw Lizzie and she asked for you, but I just shook my head.

Otherwise our life here goes on. Ben and Danny are a big help. They picked buckets and buckets of cherries, and Mamm and I baked pies, but they didn't taste as good without you here to eat a whole pie all by yourself! Danny found a bed of wild strawberries and then ate most of them before he brought them home and made himself sick. We've had some rain, so the corn grows so fast I can almost see it add inches every day. I taught Katie to make little dolls out of hollyhocks. Amos lent a hand making hay and, of all people, Crist Miller came to help. He said he'd come back in a few weeks when it's time to cut the wheat. We're hoeing tobacco every day, all of us except Katie, from sunup until we can't see anymore. Is there tobacco in Big Valley?

Well I must close for now. I pray for you every night and hope to hear from you soon.

Your loving sister,
Annie

September 29th

Dear Gideon,

I thought I would drop you a few lines to let you know about life here in the big city. I'm sorry to say that I haven't seen your sister in a long time, not since my last trip with Tateh in which we delivered the tools to your Datt and I smuggled *your letter to Annie. (I've been reading the book you so kindly left for me and have learned about all kinds of skulduggery.) I think you can imagine what it was like at your place on the day Tateh and I arrived. It was like a death in the family. Tateh delivered the tools to your Datt, who hurled them across the barnyard. I bet you're not surprised! I hope he thought better of that later and picked them up. Only Annie seemed calm and sad, but mostly calm, like a peaceful island in the midst of a stormy sea.*

I have not been back because my parents insisted that I attend classes for the rest of the summer to prepare for my bar mitzvah, and now regular school has started. I didn't enjoy the Hebrew classes, except for my friend Abie's clowning. He even convinced me to eat a piece of ham the day before the ceremony. I managed to choke it down but it came right back up again. Mameh was frantic because she thought I was coming down with something and would be sick for my bar mitzvah, but I recovered in plenty of time. It took place two weeks ago and was a great occasion. A few days later Abie did what he has been threatening to do all along and cut off his long earlocks. You can't imagine what a storm that caused. It was like a death in the family. I've decided to wait until I am out on my own and away from home before I take that step.

We are all well here. Joshua is growing fast, and Mameh's strength has returned. I hope all goes well for you in Big Valley. If you come back to visit someday, please stop to see us. I know that Sarah would be happy to have you sample some more of her cooking. Write and let us know how you are doing.

Your friend,
Isaac